1988/1990

REEF NOTES
Revisited and Revised
by Julian Sprung

Book Design by Daniel N. Ramirez

Published by Ricordea Publishing
Coconut Grove, Florida 33133

First Printing July 1995

Published by Ricordea Publishing
4016 El Prado Blvd.
Coconut Grove, Florida, USA, 33133

To purchase back issues of *Freshwater And Marine Aquarium* magazine or copies of the original "Reef Notes" articles contact:
FAMA, 144 W. Sierra Madre Blvd., Sierra Madre, CA, 91024

Printed and bound by Arnoldo Mondadori, Verona, Italy.

Design and production by Daniel N. Ramirez Design, Inc.
Cover photos by: Daniel N. Ramirez and Julian Sprung.
Fish: Scott's fairy wrasse, *Cirrhilabrus scottorum.*

ISBN 1-883693-22-5

Julian Sprung, 1966 - Reef Notes

This book is dedicated to Don Dewey and the Staff at Freshwater And Marine Aquarium magazine, whose publication initiated and propelled the reef keeping hobby in North America, and gave my column international recognition.

Acknowledgments

The following people have contributed to this book either directly or indirectly through their work and exchange of ideas: Dr. Walter Adey, Marj Awai, Stanley Brown, Dr. Robert W. Buddemeier, Roger Bull, John Burleson, Dr. Bruce Carlson, Merrill Cohen, J. Charles Delbeek, Don Dewey and the Staff at FAMA, Dr. Phillip Dustan, Svein Fosså, Anne Folan, Thomas A. Frakes, Bob Goemans, Santiago Guetierrez, Dennis Hare, Jens Krarup, Brian LaPointe, Karen Loveland, Dr. Frank Maturo, Scott W. Michael, Martin A. Moe, Jr. and Barbara Moe, Alf Jacob Nilsen, Dr. James Norris, Mike Paletta, Vince Rado, Daniel and Carmen Ramirez, Eric Sisitsky, Dietrich Stüber and the members of the Berlin Association for Marine Aquaristics, John Tullock, Dr. John Veron, and Peter Wilkens.

Table of Contents

About the Author

Julian Sprung was born in 1966 in Miami Beach, Florida. He is a graduate of the University of Florida with a Bachelor of Science degree in zoology, and is an author, consultant, and frequent lecturer on marine aquarium keeping. He has been keeping marine aquariums for over 18 years, and began studying marinelife more than 20 years ago along the shores of the island where he grew up on Biscayne Bay. Julian writes the monthly column, "Reef Notes" in *Freshwater and Marine Aquarium* magazine, on which this book is based. He has authored numerous articles in other publications such as *Seascope* and *Tropical Fish Hobbyist*, and is Science Editor for the new quarterly journal, *Aquarium Frontiers*. Julian also wrote and produced a video entitled *An Introduction to the Hobby of Reef Keeping*. In 1994 J. Charles Delbeek and Julian Sprung completed over four years of work with the publication of their book *The Reef Aquarium, Vol 1*.

Introduction

Why does a reef tank inspire so many questions? The
hunger for information seems to be the product of a
desire to achieve the perfect aquarium. A perfect reef
aquarium is not just another pretty tank. It is a living
ecosystem, thriving, growing, and ever-changing with a
diverse number of plants and animals that give it stability
and beauty. When we strive for perfect balance in a captive ecosystem our endeavor may be akin to trying to
manage a small piece of the universe, or the state of our
own existence. Aquarists develop an empathy for their
aquarium such that they too feel unhealthy when something isn't right with it. So when things get out of control
it's no wonder aquarists literally get "desperate."

Thousands of such desperate reef keepers have written,
phoned, faxed, or consulted me in the past 7 years, and I
regret that I could not respond to every request.
Fortunately, the column "Reef Notes" has afforded a powerful means of communicating to large numbers of aquarists, and I have tried to answer in my column the majority
of the types of letters I receive, to benefit those aquarists I
could not correspond with directly. The acceptance of
my column also led to numerous speaking engagements
where I had the opporunity to meet many strange and
fascinating people, and develop new friendships.

In "Reef Notes" I encourage techniques that simplify
aquarium keeping and improve the environment created. I have tried to avoid suggesting that the methods I
encourage are holy. Nevertheless at speaking engagements aquarists commonly ask me whether "I BELIEVE
IN" (ozone, 'Berlin method', live sand, algal filtration,
UV, etc.). When this is coupled with an introduction
describing me or someone else as a "guru" I wonder
whether we aquarist/authors are just hobbyists or
religious leaders. Is this a hobby or a cult?

Wondering about this I concluded that the one thing every
aquarist wants is a holy grail. The single secret pill, filter,
device, light, or whatever that solves the precise problem

experienced whether it be algae or poor health in fish or corals. We all want miracles, and we want them easy.

If there is a single thing that solves our problems it is not a magic potion, but understanding. Knowledge and the empathy that develops when we really understand the needs of the creatures we placed in our aquarium. So, if you want to succeed read my books! Don't expect me to hand you the holy grail, however. You will have to work at it, but not too hard because I promote systems that require the least fiddling and resist failure.

With this series I am enjoying the opportunity to look back at the advice I've given in my columns, offer new suggestions and revise the points where I was in error. By reviewing and revising this little bit of history, I am showing the progression of opinion regarding the proper ways to manage a reef aquarium. My column has generated some controversy over the years, as can be seen in this volume and in subsequent ones. I have always kept the door open to points of view that differ from mine because I feel that the reader should be able to see different perspectives. I have been glad that FAMA editor Don Dewey has promoted this kind of exchange.

Furthermore, I decided that since there are still some questions which remain common to this day, I want to address them separately in the appendix, where I also offer some practical tips and suggest simple aquarium set up diagrams for building a reef aquarium with low probability of mechanical and biological failure.

Finally, I want to thank Daniel Ramirez for suggesting the creation of this series based on the original "Reef Notes" column, and for his skill at designing the format and putting it all together.

Julian Sprung
May 1995

December 1988

Q. Help! What can I do about this red algae problem? It's smothering all of my invertebrates and I can't control it. As soon as I suction it off, it grows right back.
Mr. Reef, Somewhere, U.S.A.

A. Okay, so I made this one up. The problem is a real one, however, and it has been mostly mishandled in aquarium publications. The algae in question is not a true red algae, but actually a species of cyanobacteria or "blue-green" algae. There are many species, but those affecting aquaria typically form slimy mats, films, and strings, ranging in color from red to brown or deep green-black to bright green. Some very old advice which persists even to this day is that more light is needed to grow "good guy green" algae, and the bad red algae means "you don't have enough light, shame on you!" The funny thing is the "good green" algae in these aquaria is probably another blue-green algal species. The amount of light actually has little to do with the occurrence of this problem. In my experience the occurrence of a "red algae problem" is the result of an ideal nutrient supply to the algae.

Note: See appendix for step by step process to eliminate red slime algae.

Note: Calcium carbonate precipitates on the substrate. CO_2 produced by microorganisms dissolves it. Enzymes released by the cyanobacteria liberate usable phosphate which has also precipitated on the substrate.

I have seen red cyanobacteria growing in very shallow water on mud flats under intense sunlight, at moderate depths on sand under ledges, on the inside of mud-filled bottles, in nutrient-rich bays, and on nutrient-poor reefs. Quite a variety of habitats for the blue-greens, though one characteristic links them all — they always seem to grow on sediment and/or in sediment-rich areas. It is my hypothesis that cyanobacteria prefer to grown on sediment because this is where they have the most abundant food supply. They have in unlimited supply from the sediment: carbon dioxide produced by micro-organisms; ammonia produced by micro-organisms, by deamination of amino acids, and by incomplete denitrification; phosphorus bound up by, and released by, the sediment; and, if the substrate is a carbonate-based gravel, such as crushed coral, they have calcium bicarbonate formed as a precipitate on the surface of the gravel in the presence of CO_2. Many aquarists who have experimented with redox potential control have discovered that cyanobacteria can be eradicated, or at least severely limited, when the redox potential of the aquarium water is high, in the 400MV to 500MV range. It is my opinion that this is a result of starvation, as the nutrients I just mentioned are released easily under low redox potential, but their existence or release in the water is strictly limited by high redox. A better under-standing of this phenomenon is found in literature on sea-sediment interface chemistry in your public library. A further nutrient based consideration is the possibility that these algae can utilize amino acids available in the water. This might explain this ability to grow on glass or on the aquarium lid where salt-water aerosol from pop-ping bubbles may carry skimmed amino acids, phos-phorus and metals.

Back to lighting, I have observed blue-greens proliferate under every type of lighting regimen, including Metal Halide, Incandescent, Actinic, Gro-Lux™, Ultralume™, Vita-Lite™, etc. It is apparent that light is neither the cause nor the cure, though some lighting changes may enhance or inhibit growth. Some aquarists have suggest-ed a cure that involves the use of UV-emitting "black lights." Many have tried the suggestion and have been disappointed, though some report success. The UV cure stems from research which may be found in a book called *The Blue Light Syndrome* and a number of journal articles. The effect of UV light is weakened by other light's spectra present and, above all, nutrients determine whether this algae will grow or not.

I think the suggestion by Smit that establishing a dense growth of *Caulerpa* species will prevent the growth of cyanobacteria is a false hope and not a very reproducible technique. Given ideal conditions the blue-greens simply grown right on the *Caulerpa*. My own recommendations, unfortunately, are not 100% foolproof, though I offer many avenues of control. I suggest:

(1) Avoid calcium carbonate based substrates*; (2) if possible, have no sand or gravel layer in reef tanks — this will give you a naturally higher redox and allow you to siphon off detritus easily; (3) perform regular water changes using low phosphate or phosphate-free fresh water; (4) use an efficient protein skimmer; (5) do not let detritus accumulate; and (6) use a pre-filter sys-

Note: **Right from the start I was recommend-ing no substrate on the bottom. I have changed my opinion. I no longer recommend the bare-bottomed approach. Please read the intro-duction in this book and recommendations in later "Reef Notes" regarding the use of live sand.**

*Nonsense! I based my erroneous recommen-dation on an article that showed these sub-strates could lower pH. See page 6.

Other notes: **In later columns I describe the omission of mechanical filtration. Also, I am strongly opposed to the use of antibiotics, i.e. erythromycin, for the eradication of slime algae. Antibiotics harm some beneficial bacteria and create resistant strains of cyanobacteria... they are not a cure.**

By far the best cure for cyanobacteria is a combination of good protein skimming and high pH maintained with the addition of "kalkwasser"

tem which allows yo to clean it a few times per week. The use of ozone for redox control as mentioned earlier will work quite well and is worth the effort and expense, though it is not the only means of controlling problem "red algae."

Q. I'm so confused on what these new reef systems actually do! I've heard that you don't have to do water changes anymore and I cannot believe that at all. Some fish stories tell me that the dry part of the system builds bacteria that eliminates nitrates, others say that algae and live rock eliminate the nitrate. Some say that the wet part (shallow trays of coral sand) keep the pH stable, while others say it is just the regular undergravel system put outside the tank so that the aquarium looks better. Some say the return should be a steady hard pressure stream for maximum current, others say it should be a spray-bar...

A. I hope I can clear up the confusion many aquarists are feeling now with so many claims being made by aquarists having little first-hand experience with reef systems. The opinions contained in this column will be based on "hands-on" experience and research. Any rumor or second-hand knowledge will be clearly defined as such.

I have tried the range of possible water change routines. I have tried no water change (for one year), monthly 20% changes, smaller weekly changes, periodic 100% water changes, and frequent 50% water changes. I now recommend routine water changes, having never witnessed any harm done even by 100% changes, provided of course that the specific gravity and temperature of the new water are the same as the old, and the water source is reliable (i.e., no chloramine, ammonia, low phosphate, nitrate). I found that following the no-change advice eventually leads to problems with undesirable algae as a result of phosphate accumulation, and a less-than-spectacular appearance in the invertebrates — even though they can survive. When you make a change, you should notice a positive response rather quickly. My routine is to do about a 25% change per month. This is, admittedly, arbitrary. Further, regarding recommendations to do small water changes every week, I don't think it is essential to be so careful, though it never hurts.

The "dry" part of the system is the biological nitrifying filter. It converts ammonia to nitrate under very aerobic conditions afforded by the trickling action. It does not eliminate nitrate; rather, it produces nitrate. I find it interesting that you ask about "algae and live rock" removing nitrate because it is true that together they do just that. Algae do not remove nitrate directly, at least not in significant quantity to keep levels low. Algae do remove ammonia from the water (compare this with nitrifying bacteria that only convert ammonia to less toxic nitrate). In removing the ammonia the algae lower nitrate levels "from both ends." First, it is clear that pulling ammonia out of the system before it is converted to nitrate will result in a lower nitrate accumulation — this is one side of the story. Next, within the anaerobic core of the live rock, micro-organisms denitrify the accumulated nitrate in the water as well as on-site nitrate produced by nitrifying bacteria within the rock. Incomplete denitrification here may result in the formation of ammonia again, which can then be taken up by plants growing on, and in, the rock. Additionally, amino acids present in the water may be deaminated within the rock, providing more ammonia to the algae. A rock substrate affords not only a permanent base for algae, but also a tightly-held source of nutrients all in a dynamic state of flux. In a closed system with an excessive population of fish or excessive feeding, the processes just described will not maintain a low nitrate level. Partial water changes and the installation of a denitrifying filter or an algal turf scrubber can help in the case of a heavy bioload. An efficient protein skimmer and regular servicing of the pre-filter also help by removing matter that would ultimately be converted to nitrate.

The "wet" part of the system is basically a second pre-filter area to prevent clogging of the pump by the perpetual rain of bacterial slime from the dry section. It serves a minor biological function and is best made of an inert media that is easily serviced (i.e., a foam block). Gravel is undesirable because it is difficult to service. Crushed coral will not maintain your pH — actually it will work against your goal of 8.1 to 8.3, tending to bring the pH down to 8.0 or lower.

Finally, one or two "hard pressure" streams will give better current than a spray bar along the back; the smaller currents from a spraybar quickly die out as a result of friction with the reef and plants. A spraybar may be preferable in a small tank (10-20 gallons) — I have used one successfully in this situation.

References
H. Senger, ed. 1980, The Blue Light Syndrome Springer Verlag, Berlin, N.Y.

January 1989

Q. I have been a hobbyist for about 30 years but in marines about two years. I started with a 50 gallon tank then went to my 90 gallon reef system which is my pride and joy. I used FAMA's articles to help set it up and also stock it. It is a little over 8 months old now. I have around 35 invertebrates and 20 small fish. My only problem has been keeping anemones longer than 3 to 6 months. I did not do any water changes for 5 months, then Nitrates started building up so I began changing 5 gallons a week, added a skimmer 2 months ago, also ozone. Now the pH is 8.0, Nitrate .12 to .15, Nitrite .05, no ammonia. I can't seem to get the pH any higher. It has been 8.0 on my Seatest™ test kit ever since I started it. I have the "Carefree system" wet/dry sprinkler with an added Eheim 3052 inside the tank. I use 1 Actinic bulb and a muffin fan for cooling. I keep my specific gravity at 1.022, temperature at 78 to 80, hardness 15. I started using calcium supplements and vitamins by Coralife®. I also use Dupla 24 or Coralife® Iron for the *Caulerpa*. I am considering a change to Bio-balls in the filter system. I've already done this in the overflow using Tri-packs and Eheim fine and floss. I clean it once a week. I'm sending a few pictures for you to see. Thank you so much for all the good writers you have on your staff. Sincerely, Donna J. Templin, Columbus, Ohio

A. Let me say first of all that I love getting photographs! They always tell me far more than an aquarist can in a letter, and I am fascinated by the unusual specimens many aquarists have acquired and grown.

Poor success with anemones can be the result of several problems. In this example I suspect that inadequate lighting is the cause, but I will address this later. Sometimes failure with an anemone is no fault of the aquarist. Anemones often arrive from overseas looking like nothing more than a putrid jelly doughnut. Surprisingly, they recover, though recovery is often incomplete, producing substandard specimens which may seem perfectly healthy when purchased. It appears that specimens shipped with little or no water survive best.

Regarding your water parameters, 78° to 80° F is okay, but 74° to 78° is better. Prolonged exposure to temperatures above 80° in a reef aquarium is harmful to some invertebrates. You will notice that your anemones open up larger in the cooler part of this temperature range. The water change routine you now perform is good. You might see a slight improvement if you changed a full 25% of the volume at one time every few months in addition to the 5 gallons per week. Continue using your protein skimmer. Please be sure to filter the effluent from the skimmer with activated carbon to remove residual ozone. Your pH is not too bad, but the culprit of the problem and possibly other ills is the thick gravel bed evident in your photo. The best water quality is achieved when no substrate is placed on the bottom, other than live rock. The gravel will guarantee you a lower redox potential in the aquarium and, in your case, a lower pH since you have crushed coral, carbonate based, gravel (see Seascope Vol. 3, Spring 1986). I strongly suggest that you siphon this gravel bed out. If you must have something there, you can sprinkle a little silica sand near the front glass, not more than 1/4 inch. Your carbonate hardness is good. To keep it there you might periodically add SeaChem marine buffer. It is quite possible that your make-up water is able to maintain the hardness without the addition of supplements. I'm glad to see that you clean your pre-filter once a week. You have obviously learned early that reef systems are not "carefree," but well worth the effort for their beauty and interest. The more you clean your pre-filter, the less waste will accumulate and the less biological demand for oxygen. I clean mine every day. Your floss over ball media would be easy to service daily; the floss would simply be rinsed under the tap.

Regarding the proposed change to Bio-Balls, you could accomplish this by gradually removing portions of DLS,

Note: **Boy I did focus on removing substrate back then, but I was wrong...the SeaScope article points out an interesting phenomenon wherein calcium carbonate precipitates on crushed coral and the pH drops, but this process reverses as acids produced by microorganisms living in the substrate dissolve the gravel, liberating the calcium and alkalinity back into the water.**

but you haven't explained why you want to make the change. Your pre-filter should enable you to maintain the DLS indefinitely.

Back to the subject of lighting that I mentioned earlier, the minimum requirements for your tank, which I'm assuming is four feet long, would be two 4-foot 60-watt Actinics and two 4-foot 40 watt daylights, alternated Daylight-Actinic-Daylight-Actinic. Additionally, another pair of 40 watt bulbs could be added to light the back part of the aquarium where organisms are closer to the surface. This pair would be one more 40 watt daylight and a 40 watt Actinic. The two 60 watt bulbs require an 800 milliamp ballast. As mentioned earlier, your current lighting system is probably the reason for failure with some anemones — you don't have enough light.

The photo could not be reproduced. Please refer to the original column.

Comments on the photo: The *Euphyllia ancora* (upper left) will soon burn your lovely mushroom anemones and the *Scolymia* sp. behind it. Some rearrangement may be necessary. Congratulations on your prolific growth of *Halymenia floresia* (red alga, center). It is one of my favorite algae.

Q. I don't know if you have someone on your staff who can answer this or not or if you can advise me as to where to seek an answer. I would like to know if the material Perlite (as is used for potting soil) is acceptable as a biological filtration media. It would appear to be an excellent material for bacteria to grow on, but I don't know if it is chemically acceptable for fish.
Randy Blair, Las Vegas, Nevada

A. A very good question. About a year ago when I was at the University of Florida, I was talking to a fellow student who worked at the school's wastewater treatment facility about my coral reef project and wet/dry filtration. He told me that perlite had been used in water treatment, which led me to wonder about its use in aquaria. I never tried it out, but more recently when I met Norbert Tunze, he showed me the high-fired clay slag bio-granules used in his bio-reactor trickle filter. These granules are similar to Perlite on the basis of size and appearance, but do not have the negative attribute of Perlite which crumbles very easily to a white dust. Tunze's bio-granules are inert, very durable, and clean. very little media was used, but it afforded tremendous biological capacity. Perlite needs plenty of rinsing and may erode in a trickle system, though I suspect it might hold up. It certainly is very cheap. All indications are that it is inert as well. I am testing it now and will report the results in a future column. I do fear that the "dust" could injure fishes' gills. See you next month!

February 1989

Q. I have been trying for a long time now to grow *Caulerpa* in my marine tank but without success. After reading some articles in your magazine by Dr. Bloc, I thought I was onto a good thing but there is one thing he failed to clarify properly. I find that the plant does very well, some varieties in particular, for up to about six weeks, and then without any explanation it develops minute hairs on the end of the leaves (which was mentioned in the article) and then the whole plant loses its green pigment and turns transparent before dying off. He touched briefly on this point and how to combat the problem, but was rather vague. It is common to every variety of *Caulerpa* so there must be a well-known factor amongst the experts. Kevin C., Cairns, Australia

A. The phenomenon you describe is not mere death of the plant, but reproduction. *Caulerpa* species undergo what is termed anisogamous sexual reproduction. Instead of periodically shedding gametes from special structures, the entire cytoplasm of the alga is involved, becoming a reticulate network as gamete formation proceeds. An observant aquarist will notice at this point that the plant appears "blotchy." Soon small white discharge tubes called papillae grow out of the stem and erect portions of the plant, and spew out gametes and some remaining cytoplasm in a green cloud. Once the plant looks blotchy, there is no turning back. However, sometimes small sections of the plant will be unaffected. The surviving portions are often only the upright ones, without the "roots," and float free as soon as the rest of the plant disintegrates. I think that this is an alternative means of dispersal which happens simultaneously with reproduction. When I see a plant has become blotchy, I move it immediately and place it in a bucket of aquarium water. From the mass I usually recover several sections that I replant in the aquarium. I have also noticed successful growth of new "baby" plants about a month or two after total loss of a whole plant. The new growths start as hair-like projections from the rocks and soon form diminutive versions of the adult, taking months to grow into plants of normal proportions.

I wish I could offer a simple means of prevention that would work 100% of the time but I am afraid I cannot. Still, I think I can help by addressing some good and bad hypotheses that have been proposed, and suggesting some procedures you can follow to prevent the occurrence as best as possible. Hang on, this is a long one folks.

Consider that this is a natural process which can be observed along tropical coasts. I grew up on an island off Miami Beach, Florida, where I often observed large beds of *Caulerpa* die off. I grew several species of *Caulerpa* and the related genus of *Halimeda* in my aquarium and noticed the periodic die-off there as well. One very important observation I was able to make was that occasionally a plant would go into reproduction within a few days after collection and, upon returning to the collection site I discovered that the plants there were dying as well! From this we can presume two things. Either there is a time delay between stimulus and reproduction, or the plants have a biological clock. I prefer the former hypothesis, though the latter is still possible.

First I want to discuss some of the proposed hypotheses by Smit, Bloc, Thiel, and others. One concern regarded salinity as a possible culprit. Supposedly the addition of too much freshwater too rapidly would cause a change in salinity significant enough to rupture the cell wall and kill the whole plant. Too rapid a change in salinity can rupture the cell wall, but this condition is very different from the reproduction phenomenon we're concerned with. I'll dwell on this subject just a little more to add that I have observed *C. prolifera*, *C. mexicana*, and *C. paspaloides* growing in water with a specific gravity of 1.010 near freshwater springs. There are some unique areas in the Bahamas and west coast of Florida where very high concentrations of calcium ions allow marine organisms to live in very diluted seawater.

Another proposed cause for *Caulerpa* reproduction and subsequent death is a lack of sufficient CO_2. I don't believe that this is a cause, but agree that CO_2 fertilization does enhance *Caulerpa* growth. The production of CO_2 by microorganisms in the sediment and rocks, and by fish and invertebrates in the aquarium, is sufficient to supply all but the densest growth of *Caulerpa*. If the CO_2 supply runs short, however, the plant does not die. Rather, it slows down or stops growing. The use of carbonate from the water is also employed when CO_2 is used up. The common appearance of constrictions or ripples in the "leaves" of *Caulerpa* is probably produced by changes in the growth rate as a result of CO_2 supply.

Iron is yet another concern, and some aquarists believe that a shortage produces the sudden death of *Caulerpa*. Again, I cannot agree with this suggestion since there was no shortage in the natural settings, and aquarists report losing *Caulerpa* even when adding iron supplements. I am concerned that the availability of iron for plant growth is strongly regulated by redox potential, and a great deal of iron may be present in the living rock substrate therefore, even when a water test shows little or no iron. There is no question that iron is necessary for the plants, but I wonder whether aquarists' attempts to maintain a certain level in the water are as futile as a dog chasing his tail. The iron in the water can be temporarily raised, but very quickly comes out of solution. I think that plants take up iron at the interface between the substrate and the water. This is why they grow there where they can obtain an ample supply of redox regulated nutrients and CO_2.

Lack of nitrate is one suggestion which has been discussed mostly by aquarists lacking experience with growing algae. *Caulerpa* species grow best in water with next to no nitrate. They consume ammonia as a source of nitrogen. *Caulerpa* species could, therefore, be sensitive to fluctuation in available ammonia and possibly amino acids, and this could stimulate the reproduction response. I will acknowledge the possibility that other nutrients, such as phosphate, iodine, manganese, and other trace substances play a role, but it is hard to evaluate these considering the natural setting.

The next hypothesis is a good one and concerns the accumulation of organic substances which either inhibit or stimulate algae. It is quite possible that *Caulerpa* is sensitive to a threshold level of one or more organic substances in the water. My observations in aquaria support this hypothesis and the one suggesting a role of ammonia or amino acid fluctuation. I have noticed that in aquariums with protein skimmers in continuous operation, *Caulerpa* is less prone to the reproduction death syndrome. Other authors have reported just the opposite; perhaps they used skimmers intermittently.
Loss of *Caulerpa* can be compared to the trend observed in batch cultures of microalgae ("greenwater"). Typically, there is an initial rapid growth phase which can be maintained by frequent harvesting and ample supply of nutrients. If not maintained properly, the culture blooms to a peak density and crashes to nothing. The culture may periodically crash anyway, necessitating the start of a new batch with new water (accumulated organic effect). Following the analogy, one can see that frequent pruning is beneficial. Well pruned plants are more resistant to reproduction than ones left to take over the tank.

Some aquarists have noticed a correlation between high temperature and reproduction. Temperature was indeed a variable in the natural setting and I believe it relates indirectly to the next hypothesis which I am proposing, one which explains why dense beds of *Caulerpa* are more likely to go into reproduction. I think nighttime oxygen levels have a role in this phenomenon, and high temperatures, which lower dissolved oxygen, could enhance the effect. Temperature also affects the rate of reactions and functioning of enzymes, and may have a nutrient limiting effect, but I think oxygen levels are more important within normal aquarium temperature ranges. A dense growth under relatively low water flow at night could feasibly deplete the oxygen in the surrounding microlayer of water to near zero. This could very well stimulate reproduction. In fact, it would be a neat regulatory mechanism for the plant. To observe

Caulerpa's ability to deplete oxygen, one can place a mass of *Caulerpa* into a covered, small volume of water and measure the drop in oxygen concentration, by the Winkler titration method or possibly with a test kit, with a starting value at about saturation until about two or three hours incubation in complete darkness. *Caulerpa* is often shipped in a similar condition, a fact which undoubtedly leads to loss of many plants initially. You might be able to find some additional suggestions in the list of references I am providing.

References

Goldstein M. and Moral S. (1970). Gametogenesis and fertilization in *Caulerpa*. Ann. N.Y. Acad. Sci., 175, 660-72.

Graham E. (1975). Fruiting in *Halimeda* (order siphonales) 1. *Halimeda cryptica* Colinvaux and Graham. Bull. Marc. Sci., 25, 130-3.

Iyengar M.O.P. (1940). On the formation of gametes in *Caulerpa*. J. Ind. Bot. Soc., 18, 191-4.

Price, I.R. (1972) Zygote development in *Caulerpa*. Phycologia 11, 217-18.

March 1989

Q. I'd like to know how you keep sponges alive in a reef tank. I've heard that they need to be kept shaded, is this true? What do they eat? Joe Oskowiak, Windows to the Sea Club, Metuchen, New Jersey

A. Sponges are probably the most diversely colored invertebrates on the reef. Nevertheless, aquarists have been warned against the temptation to add them to their displays supposedly because they either release toxins that can kill everything, or they simply don't live very long. While there is a grain of truth in both assertions, many aquarists like myself have decided to risk tragedy, and have been rewarded with the satisfaction of growing these colorful animals.

Regarding sponges' toxicity, it is true that when damaged or mishandled some sponges release an exudate which is extremely toxic to fish. The toxic effect works several ways in an aquarium. First, if enough exudate is released, even if it is not of a toxic nature, it creates a sudden biological oxygen demand on the system which could suffocate the fish. Second, the exudate may contain toxic proteins which either bind with the gills and interfere with respiration, or which permanently injure the nervous system even upon brief exposure (pers. obs.). Of the species available to aquarists, only a few present any problem. They include the true "fire sponge," *Taedania ignis*, and the "red ball" sponge *Pseudaxinella lunaecharta*, a common import from the Atlantic. Fire sponge is a soft, dull orange to bright orange sponge that sometimes comes in with masses of the small plated cactus-like alga, *Halimeda opuntia*. A small colony of this sponge or just about any sponge for that matter, the size of a golf ball let's say, is no threat. However, a large mass can release enough exudate, if injured, to cause trouble. The red ball sponge is a beautiful bright orange sponge that is very thick and firm, usually about the size and shape of a fist. It is quite safe to keep, but I have observed newly collected and shipped specimens release a clear, slimy exudate which is toxic. They do not cause problems once established in an aquarium.

One more sponge worth mentioning here is *Chondrilla nucula*, the "chicken liver sponge." It is a dull brown, cream, mottled or dark grey sponge that has a rubbery consistency and a slimy texture. It is common on live rock and actually grows quite well in captivity. However, most of the *Chondrilla nucula* that comes on live rock dies, and when it does, it produces an unforgettable smell and a characteristic white bacterial film on the rock. This film may then spread to the boring *Cliona* sp. sponge present within most live rock, and result in an awful fouling mess. For this reason I suggest inspecting each rock in a new shipment, and removing the chicken liver sponge before it creates a problem.

Regarding lighting, it is true that many of the sponges we keep, i.e., red finger sponges, *Axinella* sp. (smooth branches, red or orange) and *Higginsia strigilata* (red, orange or yellow with bumpy branches like staghorn coral), and "cactus sponge," *Teichaxinella* sp., are collected at 30 to 90 foot depths, but they live out in the open and can be found in much shallower water. The bright purple and blue sponges, *Haliclona* sp., *Callyspongia* sp., *Dysidea* sp. occur in very shallow water in bright light. Other sponges, such as *Clathrina coriacea*, the yellow "leather latticework," occur only in the shade and will die if exposed to too much light.

I have noticed that in some sponges light is important for pigment formation. *Haliclona molitba*, a soft purple encrusting finger sponge from the Atlantic, grows purple in full sunlight, is cream colored on shaded sections under rocks, and fades to pink in dimly lighted aquaria. Light intensity is critical for many sponges. In fact, some harbor symbiotic algae like corals. The suggestion made by aquarists that sponges should always be shaded, then, is erroneous, but stems from the common problem of algae smothering the sponges and the need to prevent algal growth.

The solution to the problem of algae growing on sponges involves two conditions: Elimination of excess phosphate and the provision of proper current. Limiting phosphate is not too difficult provided the aquarist: (1) does not allow detritus to accumulate; (2) cleans the pre-filter weekly; (3) reduces the amount of substrate on the bottom of the tank;* and (4) uses phosphate-free make-up water for replacement of evaporation and for water changes. Tap water often contains a high concentration of organic phosphate which cannot easily be detected and which makes algae grow. Algae can thrive on the small amount of phosphate from daily evaporated water replacement. The use of a reverse osmosis filter on the tap water has been shown by John Burleson to eliminate this problem.

*See introduction and later comments referenced in the index about sand or other substrates on the bottom

Provision of current is critical to sponges. Most need a strong velocity of water over their surface, Without adequate current, a sponge will either suffocate very quickly and become a fouling mess, or slowly die, turning white in portions which have either suffocated or starved. Then opportunistic algae gain a foothold on the dying parts. Sponges need current to provide them with saturation levels of oxygen. The density of sponges creates a situation where oxygen is quickly depleted within them, and their fate is worsened by the fact that they are always infested by bacteria, protozoans and worms which also need oxygen. Currents stimulate the sponges to project their oscula (exhalent siphons) and thereby stimulate feeding. As the oscula (looking like clear cones) project into the current they bend, and the velocity of the passing current creates a partial vacuum which draws water out of them by Bernouilli's principle. This, in turn, brings water, oxygen, and food into the sponge through pores all over the body. A healthy sponge nearly always has projecting oscula. Healthy sponges are also able to retard algal growth by producing antibiotics and may also shed algae off with a slime coat.

The diet of sponges varies depending on the species, but most survive on a combination of bacteria, phytoplankton, and dissolved organic substances. As I said earlier, some harbor symbiotic algae which can provide food to them from dissolved inorganic substances, i.e. ammonia, just as in corals. In general, sponges can survive, grow and reproduce in aquaria, living on substances produced in the aquarium and on organisms that reproduce in the aquarium. I do not feed liquid food as I wish to maintain nutrient poor conditions as on the reef. Feeding "green water" seems like a good idea, but may only provide unwanted fertilizer to the aquarium

*I no longer agree with my old comments about pumps and plankton. in later columns I explain that pumps are not as harmful to plankton as one might expect, and the difficulty with certain sponges relates to shortage of trace elements needed to build their tissues. Phytoplankton may be a critical food for some sponge species, but it is not the pumps that cause the shortage of this food. It is the size of the aquarium.

There are still certain sponges and other invertebrates which do not survive well in a closed system. I believe success will soon be realized with these as we develop pumps and filters which are kinder to the plankton population in the aquarium.*

Had enough on sponges?

Q. First I should like to thank you for answering my last letter about mixing Actinic and fluorescent lighting. I will, hopefully, be setting up a reef system in the near future. I have been keeping freshwater fish for several years and the challenge of marine systems is irresistible. I will be setting up after my next move and that is the problem.

I will be moving to Colorado Springs, Colorado, which is at an elevation of approximately 5500 feet above sea level. My concern is whether or not the decrease oxygen carrying capacity of the water at this altitude will be conducive to keeping marine fish and invertebrates. I assume that at this atmospheric pressure there is no way, even with equipment such O_2 reactor chambers, of getting the dissolved oxygen to a saturation point closely equivalent to the animals' natural environment.

Is this a problem to be concerned with? Will the organisms thrive in this environment? Are some species more adaptable to a relatively hypoxic environment?
Michael E. Roberts, San Francisco, California

A. Well, there's an interesting question! My initial reaction to this question was to appease merely by suggesting that the pressure change would not significantly affect the oxygen concentration in the water. Then I decided I better investigate this a little more closely. After a little library research, I rediscovered a law from college physics and chemistry. I knew I had seen Henry's law before, I just never though I'd ever see it again, thank you, Michael. Henry's law simply states that the concentration of a dissolved gas is linearly proportional to the partial pressure of that gas. This was great, but I couldn't remember how of calculate the change is partial pressure of oxygen with the change in atmospheric pressure. That's where Dr. Allen Bjerkaas of Johns Hopkins University was a great help. After being told by professors at other local universities that I should ask my local pet store owner or a public aquarium about this, I finally reached Dr. Bjerkaas, who promised to call me back with an answer. He called back with a complete answer. The partial pressure of oxygen at an altitude of one mile equals **E -1/4.78** which comes out to about .81, or 81% of the partial pressure at sea level. Now, for the fish this is probably not significant. I'm sure that you could maintain a reef up there, too, but I think you need to be extra careful about not letting the oxygen level fall below saturation. I think that using an oxygen reactor, that is, a pressurized ozone contact chamber, would help raise the level of dissolved oxygen, not by inputting oxygen directly, but by oxidizing compounds that create a biological oxygen demand in the water. You should also avoid putting any sand or gravel on the bottom on the tank or in the wet section of the filter as it would deplete oxygen.* You question was certainly intriguing, and I'd really like to hear how your system works out.

*If sand is on the bottom then strong circulation in the tank is needed to insure high O_2 level.

The last question this month is another one by "Mr. Reef, somewhere, U.S.A." A number of aquarists have asked me in phone conversations about lateral line disease. I still attribute this malady to diet and water quality as I did in an article and letter in this magazine about six years ago. I am writing about this now as I recently discovered a convenient source for the cure, at Oriental markets, of all places. Oriental markets, particularly Korean ones, often have fresh seaweed stored in a brine solution. They also have numerous species of algae, fish and shrimp in freeze-dried form. The stuff is reasonably priced, too. Feeding tangs and angels the fresh algae should cure them provided water quality is not the irritant.

One more topic before the conclusion. The question of substances being produced by plants and inverts which help cure disease and prevent its occurrence has been raised a number of times in this magazine. I do believe that antibiotics released into the water by plants and inverts have a beneficial effect on fish. For further information on this subject, see the two sources I am providing at the end of this column. I will have more to say about the subject of disease and fish in reef tanks next month. See you then.

References
Burkholder, Paul R. (1973). Ecology of Marine Antibiotics and Coral Reefs. In O.A. Jones and R. Endean (eds.), *Biology and Geology of Coral Reefs, Vol. 2,* Academic Press, New York.

Scheuer, P.J. (1987), Bioorganic Marine Chemistry. Springer-Verlag, New York.

April 1989

Last month I provided a couple of references on the subject of antibiotics and drugs produced by marine organisms. I also promised to discuss fish disease in reef systems, and I will do that after the questions this month.

Q. I have recently read several articles that claimed that keeping *Goniopora* species such as Moon, Star, Flower and Sunflower is very difficult. The limit seems to be less than six months. Do you have any suggestions and/or hints on keeping this beautiful coral alive for an extended period of time (two years or more)? Regards, Joseph

E. Oskowiak, Abington, Pennsylvania

A. Wow, Joe, two months in a row you're in FAMA! Of course, I have suggestions. The genus *Goniopora* contains a number of very lovely species with unusual polyps that project several inches beyond their calyces on a rounded base. This coral has been imported for many years and has the endearing attribute of looking fabulous for several months and suddenly falling ill. This attribute makes it a great selling item; a combination of beauty and mystery that makes you want to keep on trying and keep on buying. A number of factors (i.e. temperature, lighting, and water movement) contribute to poor success with this or any other species of coral, though this one I think presents a problem even for the "experts." I would not put a limit of six months on *Goniopora,* though, as I have witnessed many that have done well for longer than a year. Still, after about a year, most *Goniopora* specimens in captivity no longer extend their polyps as magnificently as when first obtained. Many specimens then begin to die, gradually receding from the skeleton until very little coral remains. Some specimens appear to survive without deteriorating, though they no longer fully extend their polyps. I know of only one success with this genus, and that is at the Waikiki Aquarium. When I visited Bruce Carlson there about six years ago, he showed me some very large specimens which he had kept for several years. They were all thriving, and some had recovered from serious infections which Bruce cured by dipping the affected areas in freshwater. It is difficult to assess the secret to the success at Waikiki since the specimens received natural sunlight and frequent water exchange with filtered natural seawater. I'd like to add, for the benefit of those who suspect food deprivation, that Bruce does not feed his corals, and that the seawater used in his original aquaria did not contain zooplankton. The possibility of a trace chemical requirement exists, but I doubt this is the problem.*

Now I will add my own biased and hypothetical two cents. I believe the secret at Waikiki was mostly due to the water exchange, through clearly natural sunlight is far superior to any artificial light source. Unfortunately, this does not lead to the simple solution of performing more water exchanges to achieve success with *Goniopora.* I

*Success with *Goniopora* has improved over the years since this column was written, but it is still a mysteriously difficult coral. I now believe that trace elements do play an important role in the problem. Also, lighting seems to be a factor, but general statements cannot be made since different species have different requirements. There is also speculation about the importance of amino acids in nutrition See: "Coral Nutrition," Part I, II, and III by Dana Riddle *FAMA* April, May, and June 1994.

think the key lies in the dilution of accumulated organic phosphate afforded by exchanges with water poor in this nutrient. Tap water often contains both organic and inorganic phosphate, so that water exchanges may compound the problem. Phosphate test kits, by the way, give a misleading result since it is possible to have no inorganic phosphate present (the test shows "no phosphate") while there is plenty of organic phosphate there. I realize that I have blamed this source for other ills, but it is all with sound reason. Phosphate is a poison in the calcification process, and calcification is believed to be enhanced when phosphate is removed from the site of calcium deposition. You may be getting ahead of me by realizing now that Zooxanthellae, the symbiotic algae that live within coral's tissues, play a key role in calcification not only in the removal of CO_2, but also in the removal of phosphate. In this way, having less that perfect lighting and excess organic phosphate presents a compound problem, and I believe this is what happens in many aquaria. This is probably one reason shy corals recede from the skeleton when lighted improperly.

As I have emphasized in the past, control of phosphate is accomplished by using a reverse osmosis filter on the tap water, performing water changes and evaporation make-up with R.O. water, preventing the accumulation of detritus, cleaning the pre-filter often, and with the use of an efficient protein skimmer. In addition, algae filtration shows a tremendous benefit here, and the use of wave surge can help by keeping detritus suspended so that it can be trapped by the pre-filter.

I am presenting this hypothesis linking phosphate with poor success keeping *Goniopora* before actually completing any experiments to show otherwise. While on the subject of phosphate hypotheses, I'd like to present another related one which concerns a cryptic little green alga called *Ostreobium* that bores into the skeleton of living corals. Biologists have puzzled over its function and could find no definite purpose for its being there. I think it might play an important role in phosphate regulation and may aid calcification.*

When attempting to keep *Goniopora* there are some

*This hypothesis has not been substantiated. In fact, *Ostreobium* may harm the coral since it bores through the skeleton, thus weakening the structure. Elevated phosphate and/or nitrate can stimulate proliferation of this alga throughout the coral skeleton. Wilkens, (1990) proposed that this may be one cause of failure with Goniopora.

additional parameters that should be maintained to achieve best success. Temperature is critical for hard corals; *Goniopora* likes water currents and should be bathed by a good turbulent flow. Wave surge would be a plus too. Finally, lighting is key to success. *Goniopora* is a misleading coral because it responds positively to most lighting initially, even to metal halide lights which ultimately burn back its tentacles.* I recommend the proper intensity of a combination of Actinic and Daylight fluorescent bulbs, just as I recommend for all hard corals. Please note that intensity is very important. I am providing a chart as a guide for lighting typical sized aquaria (Table 1). Here are some other considerations about *Goniopora*. *Goniopora* usually grows in large monospecific stands, and the specimens we receive are often hacked off of a columnar base and may therefore be injured. More importantly, considering their typical isolation in mature, this genus may be sensitive to the slime exuded by other coral species. It may be a problem of *Goniopora* being stung or irritated by other coral in the aquarium even when they do not touch and attack each other.

I would be very interested to hear from anyone with additional hypotheses concerning this genus, especially anyone growing this coral under natural sunlight in a closed system.

Q. There seems to be some confusion over the use of the Actinic 03 bulb in my area. Although everyone agrees on its usefulness in keeping reef systems thriving, I cannot get my local dealer to agree on a few things.

First of all, there seems to be some disagreement as to whether the Actinic 03 sheds some UV along with its primarily blue spectrum, and whether this bulb would be hazardous to the human eye.

Secondly, we who have reef systems with fish tend to wonder if keeping the Actinic 03 on at night only, to avoid any UV exposure to the eye while benefitting the reef system, would stress the fish due to a constant light source being in the tank, even though the intensity of the Actinic 03 is low. May we please have an expert

*Wow, can you believe I said that? At the time I noticed what I called "burning" in corals under metal halide, which was a subject full of controversey. In fact, shortage of trace elements and the production of excess oxygen by the high rate of photosynthesis under high intensity lighting was the cause for the "burn" appearance. The bulbs were not at fault!

Table 1

Recommended Lighting for Typical-sized Aquariums:

50 gal   48"x13"x20"
(2) - 4' 60w Achnic &
(2) - 4' 40w Daylight

70 gal   48"x18"x20"
(2) - 4' 60w Actinic &
(2) - 4' 40w Daylight
    and optional
(1) - 4' 40w Actinic &
(1) - 4' 40w Daylight

90 gal   48" long,
            same as 70 gal tank
(3) - 4' 60w Actinic
(3) - 4' 40w Daylight

125/135 &150 gal 72" long
(2) - 5' 140w Actinic &
(2) - 6' 85w Daylight or
(2) - 6' V H O Daylight

30 gal   36" long
(4) - 2' 40w Actinic &
(2) - 3' 30w Daylight

Note: When Philips begins to manufacture 3' Actinics, 36" tanks will be easier to light. Also, the bulbs should be alternated (i e, Actinic/Day/Actinic) and staggered for best results. 4' 60w and 2' 40w Actinic require 800 mA ballast (HO). 5' 140w Actinic requires 1500 mA ballast (VHO).

* Some definitions of UV include light up to 400 nm. VHO & HO actinics have some output at 380 nm.

opinion so that we may put these questions to rest?
George Haritonovich, Lakewood, Ohio

A. At the time I received this letter I had been getting literally several phone calls per day asking the same question, from all over the U.S. and Canada. It is truly remarkable how rumors spread throughout the hobby and aquarium industry. I even received a call from someone who was preparing an article on the subject. I saved him some embarrassment when I informed him (listen up everyone) that Actinic 03 bulbs do not emit UV light, no UV light, none, period. I am providing a spectral chart which shows the output of the Actinic 03 UV light. Both long- and short-wave occurs up to a wavelength of 380 nanometers. The output of the Actinic 03 is zero at 380 nm, and peaks at 420 nm. I must add that the source of the rumor about the bulbs is probably its own manufacturer, Philips, who incorrectly described the Actinic 03 as UV emitting in the catalog and information sheet on the bulb. I have positive confirmation from Philips that the text about the bulb was in error, that the chart is correct, and that no UV is emitted.* By the way, these bulbs are used in hospitals to treat infants with jaundice. If you still need the assurance of someone who knows the bulb, please contact North American Philips Lighting Corporation. I do not recommend running the Actinic bulbs at night.

Recent experimentation by John Burleson using reverse osmosis filtered tap water have shown that it is an effective inhibitor for the growth of diatoms. Diatoms, or "golden brown algae," typically form a brown rust-like film on the glass and are generally disliked by aquarists because they grow so quickly and fog up the view. R.O. filtered tap water not only limits algae nutrients such as nitrate and phosphate which the diatom needs, but it also removes a more critical nutrient, silicate. The use of reverse osmosis filtered tap water effectively reduces maintenance by extending the period between cleanings of the viewing glass.

How about a new hypothesis concerning the symbiotic relationship between clownfish or crustaceans and sea anemones? I think the anemone benefits in having an

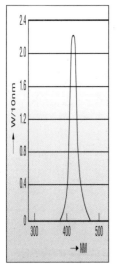

Table 2
Absolute Spectral Power Distribution of 'TL' 40W/03 RS Lamp

Please see appendix for suggested cure for ich in reef aquaria.

on-site source of ammonia (nitrogen) and carbon dioxide to feed its Zooxanthellae.

Finally, we come to the topic of disease in reef tanks. Much controversy has been generated among "old salt" aquarists concerning the claims by reef keepers that fish are healthier in reef tanks and that they may show dramatic cures without medication. I wish to add to the topic that I have experienced the same remarkable cures and fish health in my reef aquaria, but that I have also witnessed many very sick fish in reef tanks. No miracles are involved here. Some answers may be found in the list of references I provided last month. So many of the plants and animals we keep in our reef tanks leach out potent antibiotic substances to ward off predators, disease, fouling organisms, and competitors for space. I do believe that these substances plan a role in preventing fish disease. Of course, reef aquaria offer the possibility of a more natural diet for some fish, and this certainly contributes to better health. I have noticed that certain less common disease problems persist in our aquaria. For instances, I have seen both "black spot" (turbellarian) disease and parasitic worms overcome and kill individual fish in reef aquaria. The problems did not spread, by the way, but the fish were not safe from death because they resided in a reef tank.

Many hobbyists have asked me about "that one damned fish that I can't catch" which has an unshakable case of ich while all the other fish are perfectly healthy. I have had that fish too, and there is a certain danger involved in keeping him since the elevated number of parasites generated by his perpetual infection may ultimately weaken the other fish though, surprisingly, this usually doesn't happen. There may be a few reasons for the "one-fish-ich syndrome," but typically it is a result of continual harassment by other fish. Still, some fish simply seem to have a lower resistance to ich. Many aquarists have reported to me that tangs fall in this category. I still must agree with the "old salts" that fish should be quarantined, even for reef aquaria. I seldom follow this advice, however, and this fact has cause the unnecessary death of a few fish.

Some things must be controlled in all marine aquaria to

prevent disease problems. Temperature is probably the most critical factor in the incidence of ich, in my experience. The temperature should be maintained stable and below 80° F for best success. Thick gravel beds create a huge oxygen demand on the system which can stress fish; they may also release doses of Hydrogen Sulfide that can be lethal or chronically toxic. The fluctuations of pH that occur in reef tanks utilizing carbonate gravels is still one more persistent stress that can be avoided by using inert media only. Finally, fish in reef aquaria seem to exhibit heightened territoriality, so the aquarist must either carefully choose specimens or get lucky.

Next month I will discuss fish trapping techniques, among other things. See you then.

May 1989

Q. It seems that the reef style aquarium systems are taking the world by storm. The concept of maintaining a small ecosystem in your living room is indeed an intriguing one. Having been a hobbyist for some time I am always on the lookout for new things to do, so naturally I am interested in setting up a reef tank. However, I have two questions which I hope you can answer. (1) What is the minimum size a reef tank should be? (2) If everyone wants to have a piece of the "reef pie" will there be any left for nature? How is the aquarium trade dealing with the demand for live rock? Have we learned to preserve nature and take only what can be safely taken without affecting the environment, or are we recklessly stripping the ocean of her treasure just to satisfy our hobby?

Could you tell me the state of our reefs and the effect the live rock demand has had on these delicate ecosystems? I hope that aquarists have learned from the past and realize w must be somewhat prudent and preserve for the future . . . the aquariums we keep are of little importance if we ruin nature in the process. Sincerely, Markus Baer, Langley, B.C., Canada

A. Thank you, Markus, for a couple of good questions. Minimum tank size? There is none! Small tanks do have some limitations in the selection of specimens of considerable size, though. Some purists may hold that larger tanks are more stable than small ones and are, therefore, easier to maintain. More water does afford better stability with respect to parameters such as temperature and pH, but I consider smaller tanks easier to maintain on several accounts. First, given the proper dimensions, a smaller tank can be easier to light because of its shallow depth (height). In a smaller tank, a 25% water change is relatively inexpensive. Removal of detritus in a small tank can be accomplished simply with the periodic use of a diatom filer. This would be impractical in a large aquarium It is also easier to perform experiments in a smaller closed system. I like small tanks because they allow the creation of truly miniature coral reefs. The visual effect of many small delicate and colorful varieties of invertebrates all mixed in a detailed little collage can be more captivating than the otherwise breathtaking displays of giant specimens in a large tank.

The heart of your question concerns me, too, and I'm glad that you brought it up. In the years that I have been experimenting with captive reef systems, I have found that the best environment is created when all living rock is used, rather than dead "base" rock with a skin of living ones. The origin of the rock, in addition, makes a significant difference. May reef tanks have been established using shore rock collected either in the Florida Keys or along Florida's West coast. The rock collected onshore is typically fossilized limestone and is very dense (heavy). It is also typically coated with a variety of lovely algae including *Padina, Laurencia, Sargassum, Jania, Acetabularia, Acanthophora* and *Caulerpa* if it is from the Keys, and *Gracilaria, Ulva, Sargassum, Ceramium, Codium,* and *Caulerpa* if it is from the Gulf of Mexico further north. The growth of coralline algae typical of the reef environment is sparse and is represented mostly by *Fosliella* which is more tolerant of the higher nutrient inshore environment. This rock is the poorest choice for building the reef because it is not much different from dead base rock with a thin coating of living plants and animals. In time many aquarists discover that some of their shore rock has a base of cement or asphalt. Geologically speaking, shore rock is either very ancient or very new! Removal of this type of live rock probably does not affect the environment significantly, though if its mass is not replenished with rock additions, certain shoreline habitats could be smothered by sediments on a small scale.

Since 1989 there has been legislation in the state of Florida banning the collection of live rock in state waters and much debate about the collection of live rock from federal waters. The collection of natural live rock from North Carolina to Texas from state and federal waters will end after 1986. Only aquacultured rock from special bottom leases will be allowed to be collected. Collectors have begun planting huge quantities of rock at leased bottom sites. I believe the quantity planted already exceeds what was ever collected. See Delbeek and Sprung, 1994 *The Reef Aquarium, Vol 1*.

Another source some of the rock aquarists are using to build their reefs is hardbottom reefs far offshore in the Gulf of Mexico. These too are ancient limestone and are very dense. Green, sponge-like *Codium* sp. and thick-branched red *Eucheuma* sp. are characteristic algae on these rocks which are also "painted" by exquisite pink, red, and purple coralline algae, particularly if the rock originates from deep water. This rock is a reliable source of *Halymenia floresia*, a brilliant red jagged edged algae with a slippery texture. Small growths of the corals *Astrangia* sp., *Cladocora arbuscula*, *Siderastrea radians*, and *Oculina diffusa* are also common on this rock, as are colorful sponges, tunicates, and bryozoans including a blood-red *Stylopoma* sp. and lacy branched *Caulibugula*. Deep water rock from the Gulf of Mexico is a good choice for building the reef, though the abundant rubbery chicken-liver sponge, *Chondrilla nucula*, should be removed to prevent fouling. The hardbottom areas where these rocks originate are unique northern outposts of tropical and subtropical reef fauna. While removal of the organisms is not ecologically significant because the areas are extremely rich and productive, removal of the rock is significant because it is no longer being built up at a rapid rate.* I am concerned that some of these areas could be adversely affected, though they are extensive enough to be harvested for many years without noticeable effects. Consider that most of the rock taken is merely loose rubble on top of a base of more rubble and hardbottom.

*I may have been incorrect. The coralline algae there actually do grow quickly and they consolidate and cement the sand into rocks.

Still another source of live rock is in completely tropical hardbottom areas. One of these is located along the Gulf Coast of the Florida Keys where most of the *Ricordea florida* or "false coral" rock is collected. This rock makes a nice top decoration, but is a poor choice for building as the coralimorpharians need light and because the rock is characteristically overgrown with a lot of chicken-liver sponge. The other collecting area is a source of "gold" in my opinion. Hardbottom and patchy reef areas along Florida's east coast produce some of the nicest rock for building the reef. This rock is usually coated, top and bottom, with pink, red, and purple crustose coralline algae, while the upper surface has macro-algae growth including *Dasycladus vermicularis*, *Udotea* sp., *Valonia ventricosa*, *Halimeda discoidea*, *Caulerpa* spp., *Dictyota* and *Dictyopteris* sp., *Laurencia* sp., and *Galaxaura* sp., among others. Although the patchy reefs stretch for a couple of hundred miles along the coast, they are only a few hundred yards across in many areas. Some of these communities undergo cyclical burial and unearthing as a result of shifting sediments, and are often stressed by extremes of temperature in summer and winter. They are still healthy, nevertheless, having withstood the recent dredge and fill heavy siltation around Miami Beach and Hollywood. Though I know that these areas are extensive, I have been concerned that the removal of mass, though it exposes still more rubble, is a risky practice that should be accompanied by rock replenishment using suitable (limestone) substrate. I have recently been pleased to be informed that rock collectors are now doing just that now in Florida and in Hawaii.

I have wondered in addition how the interest in living aquaria has affected the sales of dead bleached coral. The killing of large coral heads for the sake of decoration now affects me emotionally. These structures are not so easily replaced as rocks.

Some of the live rock is coming out of the Sea of Cortez and Hawaii. I am unfamiliar with the terrain in the Sea of Cortez and have not seen much of this rock. Hawaiian rock is interesting because of its distinctive shape. It is basically the overgrown skeletons of a species of *Porites* (finger) coral and looks like fused branches. Some consider it the best rock, though I prefer rock from Florida and the Caribbean.*

Q. I've had my present reef set up for about a year. I started it with all live rock from Hawaii. A few months ago I added a couple of pieces from the Caribbean.

*Collection of live rock from Hawaii ended back in 1989 and other sources opened up, including Indonesia, Tonga, the Marshall Islands, Fiji, Pohnopei, and the Solomon Is. After years of setting up tanks with different types of rock I prefer Fiji, Indonesia, and Gulf of Mexico rock. These have the most beutiful and hardy coralline algae.

Since then I've had an outbreak of green hair algae. Two questions: (1) Have you noticed that Hawaiian rock doesn't produce the hair algae? (2) How do I get rid of this hair algae? Thank you for your support,
Wyn Belorusky, Jr., San Antonio, Texas

A. No, I haven't noticed the connection, but I have a pretty good idea why you have, and I'll explain shortly. First, the term "green hair algae" refers to a number of species, and a description of photograph would have helped a little. (Hang on folks, there's more Latin names to follow.)

The addition of live rock to an established aquarium is typically followed by a bloom of two types of algae: Brown diatoms which quickly coat the glass, and bushy green *Bryopsis plumosa* or *Bryopsis pennata* which are similar in appearance to "hair algae," but careful observation reveals feather or fern-like tips (Bry = fern, opsis = like). These blooms may completely envelop the rocks initially, but will usually "crash" so that *Bryopsis* and Diatoms later grow only in small patches or not at all. A later addition of live rock will bring on another bloom, which is really a minor problem compared with the risk of fouling created by late additions of a large quantity of fresh rock.

The hair algae which make aquarists tear out their own hair include: *Cladophora, Cladophoropsis, Chaetomorpha, Enteromorpha, Derbesia marina, Boodleopsis,* and *Caulerpa fastigiata.* Some of these are easily described like *Bryopsis. Cladophora* and *Cladophoropsis* include many species that form bushy green turfs of hair-like filaments that are coarse in texture, somewhat like a Brillo Pad. They are distinctive in having many cross-walls which give the hairs a banded appearance under the microscope or upon close inspection. *Enteromorpha* forms tufts of tubular green filaments, and, like *Bryopsis,* usually blooms and "crashes." *Caulerpa fastigiata* forms dark green turfs and is distinguished by the rhizome-like or "root" structures that are characteristic of the other members of this genus. *Derbesia marina* is the suspected identity of the beast that plagues more aquaria than any other algae. It is dark green, turf forming and soft in texture, the filaments being occasionally branched with a slight constriction at the junction of a branch. These constructions are noticeable only under the microscope. The distinction between *Derbesia* and *Boodleopsis* is poorly defined in the literature that I have read, and the experts I have consulted have left me only weakly confident that *Derbesia marina* is the real problem hair algae.

At any rate, you asked how to get rid of the stuff and fortunately I have a solution for you! Follow the advice I gave in my column about "red slime algae" since the requirements of green hair algae and *Cyanobacteria* appear to be much the same. In fact, they usually occur together in our aquaria. You may employ snails such as *Astraea tectum*, limpets or some *Turbo* sp. now available to hobbyists — they do a marvelous job, but your ultimate goal should be to eliminate sources of organic phosphate (there I go again). Read on.

The brown stuff could also be a dinoflagellate. Please see the appendix for info about dinoflagellates.

Q. Since we are new at keeping mini-reefs, we set up a small 29 gallon system to try our luck. We are having wonderful success with anemones, corals, feather dusters, etc. Some animals have doubled in size in less than three months. Our problem is not being able to get any green algae or other plants to grow. Brown and wine-red algae covers everything. The wine-red algae looks almost like a piece of velvet. Plants like *Caulerpa* are completely coated with brown algae in just a few days with no signs of green showing through, then die off. Some of the enveloping brown algae has lots of air bubbles in it (is that good or bad) all the time. We assume it is correct to siphon out some of this algae from time to time. How do we get green? Thank you, Stuart Price, Watertown, New York

A. The water in Watertown ain't so good. The velvet algae you describe is a Cyanobacteria or "blue-green" algae, even though it is wine-red. The brown slime is either another blue-green, or a diatom which blooms in the presence of excess silicate from your tap water. I discussed red slime algae in my first column in this magazine. The cause of its growth is the accumulation of organic phosphate, especially in the presence of calcium carbonate-based gravel or sand (crushed coral, calcite, dolomite, oyster shell). I disagree with aquarists who

Wow, another time I goofed with the advice to remove bottom substrate. I was wrong, but it is common experience to develop slime algae on newly added bottom sand or gravel. This is remedied with tiny herbivorous hermit crabs, strong water currents, and the maintenance of high pH with kalkwasser additions.

It is true that phosphate ends up in the substrate, but it also ends up in the rocks, so removing the sand is not the answer.

*Actually, water treatment plants sometimes add organic forms of phosphate to the water to prevent buildup of minerals in pipes. These organic phosphates do not give a reading on a simple phosphate test kit which only reads inorganic phosphate.

persist in the erroneous assumption that these substrates are essential, but that is another subject which I'll cover next time. Organic phosphate sticks to the gravel which absorbs it like a sponge, and which becomes a storage zone. Organic phosphate in the presence of calcium stimulates the Cyanobacteria's "phosphate activity." What these little buggers do is to release enzymes (phosphatases) across their cell membrane that slice phosphate off of the organic molecules. This whole process works best in the presence of excess calcium which is easily obtained from calcium bicarbonate that precipitates onto the surface of carbonate gravels. (This is why you may notice white powder under your velvet!) This is also one reason which I advise: (1) Avoid carbonate gravels; (2) avoid sand and gravel because they hold all phosphates; and (3) do not allow detritus to accumulate.

Perhaps the most significant source of organic phosphate is the tap water. Treatment plants effectively remove inorganic phosphate, but often leave a fair amount of the organic fraction.* Daily make up for evaporation supplies all the food these guys need. The use of an inexpensive reverse osmosis filter on the tap will effectively eliminate this problem. Distilled water, by the way, is not a substitute since some organic compounds may boil before water and be rinsed along with water down the condenser. Bottled distilled water also may contain a very high level of copper from copper tubing used in cheaper stills — beware!

The air bubbles you notice are oxygen produced by the algae. These are neither good nor bad. They are just a sign that photosynthesis is occurring. You should siphon the algae away until you can get it under control with a reverse osmosis filter.

My goodness, I almost forgot I was supposed to talk about fish traps. Ritchie Rothowski of the "Windows to the Sea" club called recently to describe a trap that worked for him. It should work for at least some of you! Basically, Ritchie attached a cone shaped piece of black DLS material to the mouth of a large jar and baited the trap with a little food. A plastic funnel with a properly sized opening cut into it would work as well. Ritchie

There are now several types of traps commercially available to aquarists. Ask your dealer.

swears it wasn't long before he had a jar full of fish!

Other aquarists have resorted to fashioning miniature Hawaiian slings that work well but, unfortunately, produce fatal catches. Many traps have been devised, most on the same theme of a baited vessel that the fish easily enters but never leaves. I would gladly present hobbyists' designs in a future column. Next time I will discuss mantis shrimp traps. The "Windows to the Sea" newsletter described an interesting one, and I have come up with some other ideas of my own. See you then.

June 1989

This month we continue with the subject of live rock, and after a couple of questions, Ill discuss my views on the question of calcite and other buffer media. Of course, I'll also cover mantis shrimp trapping techniques as promised.

Q. I am going to use dead coral as a base for my live rock. Is this a good idea or do you have a better idea? How often and how much live rock can be put in at one time? Thank you, Rick C. Tyler

A. There are many questions which don't have a clear-cut yes or no answer, and your first one is one of these. I can tell you that my usual response to this question is that using dead base rock won't result in some horribly disastrous explosion, and it is true that invertebrates and algae will spread and colonize the "new territory," but I still prefer to create a reef tank using all living rock. It is not true that underlying rocks "will die anyway" as I have heard many uninformed hobbyists preach. Good quality rock will have encrusting sponges and coralline algae that will proliferate beneath, and between, the rocks. It is hard for me to explain exactly why I prefer to use all living rock considering that recolonization occurs, but I'll give it a shot. First, each live rock you purchased already has been colonized by an enormous variety of bacteria, protozoans, invertebrates, and algae, while a mere fraction of these are manifest as a result of the particular environmental conditions (temperature, light and water movement, nutrient supply, etc.) that existed where the rock was collected. Each rock, therefore, has a potential to produce a lot of life. The less live rock you use, the lower that potential production is, and the colonization onto other rocks which occurs is limited to far fewer species that can exist on a single live rock. I have noticed that aquaria using all live rock have a greater variety of algae and invertebrates, and that the source of the rock (shore versus reef) makes a significant difference in the ultimate captive reef produced. Finally, I suspect that starting out with all live rock has a further advantage in the production of an actual plankton cycle involving bacteria, protozoans, algae, crustaceans, various invertebrate larvae, as well as invertebrate-generated detritus and plant detritus with attached bacteria and protozoans. This cycle is natural and perpetual and, in my opinion, sufficiently meets the needs of most filter feeding invertebrates without the need for supplemental additions. Every reef keeping aquarist has his or her own recipe for adding rock to the aquarium. Naturally, I have my own method, and it should stand to reason that mine is the best method since I think so, understand? In answer to your question, the live rock should all be added at one time. The best way to do this is to use live rock which has been maintained in a rock holding system for three weeks or more without any lighting. During this period decaying algae, sponges, etc., will be dumped off the rock and broken down, and much of the excess sand and detritus will be expelled. It is best not to light the rocks to prevent undesirable algae from gaining a foothold when the nutrient levels are higher. It is not essential to have such a rock holding system as the rocks may be kept unlighted this way in the display tank. When fresh live rock is received, each rock should be carefully cleaned by vigorous shaking in saltwater (never ever put a live rock in freshwater) and stripping off all macroalgae. I do not recommend scrubbing the rocks as common practice since I believe that many desirable species could be lost this way. Scrubbing is only useful in the incidence of fouling. As a point of interest, most of the algae species stripped off by hand will grow back under the proper conditions, even if the rocks are kept in the dark initially for many months.*

*If the rock is fresh and the algae is not excessive or rotting, it can be left alone (don't strip off plating red coralline algae) and of course the rock can be illuminated. Rocks with zoanthids or coral-limorphs (i.e. *Ricordea florida*) definitely should be illuminated. Some aquarists misunderstood my recommendations here, which were for those rocks used to build the reef structure on which one wants to encourage proliferation of coralline algae.

Some other points of interest: I do not recommend adding the rock in stages since it is potentially a harmful technique if fish or invertebrates are already established.

Here is where I began to hint that one could set up a reef tank minus a wet/dry filter.

Starting out with a filter that has been seeded using ammonium chloride before the rocks were purchased probably offers the greatest margin of safety. Nevertheless, I have witnessed many set-ups in which seeded live rock (this refers to rock which has been held in an established tank for three weeks or more) was used, the filter being new and unseeded, and these instant aquaria showed no rise in ammonia or nitrite. It appears that many authors have overlooked the tremendous potential biological surface offered by live rock. Finally, many of the specimens we add to the aquarium after the initial rock installation are growing on pieces of live rock. The addition of a few of these does not present a problem.

Q. First of all let me congratulate you. While I was at the University of Florida I was an avid aquarium keeper and had heard many things about your ability. I am glad to see that your work has culminated in the level of recognition you deserve. Now to my questions. My hobby has been on hold for the past three years while I am finishing my doctoral work at Texas A&M. When I finish this year, I hope to set up a reef tank. I have been looking at the dry filter materials: Bioball, Tripack, DLS, etc., and I am overwhelmed by the price. I cannot understand why (with a sufficient prefilter) a series of thin filter plates — like air filters from a standard home hot air furnace — cannot be used. These filters could be set up in a number of layers, with air between, and it seems to me from their fibrous nature they would have a very high surface area. I am very interested in your reaction to this. Sincerely, Joe Signorile

A. Wonder why I chose to print this letter? Thanks for the almost embarrassing compliment! Regarding your question, Joe, you seem to have a pretty good idea there, somewhat along the lines of Dr. Blok's DLS or Jurgen Lemkemeyer's surface filter. It is true that you would have very high surface area using floss trays or screens, but the source you chose, and the reason you chose it, I must warn you against. I guarantee you that hot air furnace filter plates are treated with a fire retarding substance, something you just can't take a chance with since it could leach out into the water and produce long term problems. Let me now warn you and other aquarists with a phrase my mother taught me when I was very young. "Cheap is dear!" she said, and you know she was right. While I strongly encourage tinkerers to experiment and build to their heart's desire, I must draw the line when the aquarist tries to do something because it's cheaper, and disregards quality and long term success and happiness. In your case, we're not taking about much of a difference in cost — if you want a DLS type media, buy DLS — it is not very expensive either pre-rolled, or by the foot, for the materials. I am glad that you are very aware of the need to have a "sufficient prefilter." Good luck with your work at Texas A&M, and let me know how the reef turns out.

Q. I have a 75 gallon reef tank in my office that is 20" deep with four fluorescents, 48" long. Will you please publish a comment telling your readers at what distance from the lights various anemones should be placed? Also, what is the best way to feed them — shove food down their throats, or put it in the petals? Will they absorb more if you feed them just before turning out the lights, or in the morning? How often? Conrad Leslie

A. Have you hugged your anemone today? I don't know if I should call the A.S.P.C.A. or what?! First of all, let's get a couple of things straight. Anemones don't have throats or petals. They have a pharynx and tentacles. Now, regarding your question about location with respect to lighting, my first inclination is to tell you that anemones have a habit of correcting your errors in judgment by simply moving to a more suitable location. If you own a *Radianthus ritteri* you may find that the proper location doesn't exist at all, but that somewhere on the front glass is a close second. It is hard to recommend an exact placement because each individual anemone's requirements vary depending on where it occurred on the reef, and how long it has been receiving inadequate sunlight in captivity. I suspect, by the way, that your aquarium does not have enough intensity of light. Some other anemone-like animals, such as "mushroom anemones" and zoanthid anemones ("sea-mat," *Palythoa* species, and "yellow polyps") are more specific in their requirements. Mushroom anemones, which are actually more closely related to stony corals, also vary in their lighting require-

Note: Radianthus ritteri is the common trade name for Heteractis magnifica.

ments based not so much on species, but on how long they have been inadequately lighted.They occasionally have a difficult time adapting to a change in light (spectrum and intensity), but most often fare best when first placed toward the bottom of the aquarium in the light. They may be gradually moved up. I have observed numerous species of mushroom anemones growing on the underside of ledges when diving. Zoanthid anemones are generally best placed higher up in the tank. If the lighting is good, they do well just about anywhere in the tank, but they seem to like really intense light.

It is now my opinion that occasional feeding is beneficial. We now maintain such good water quality with protein skimming and the use of live rock and sand that the food does not cause a pollution problem. It is good to feed anemones at least once per month with small pieces of shrimp or fish.

Regarding feeding, it is my opinion that photosynthetic anemone fare best when you don't feed them. While certain nonphotosynthetic Cnidarians, i.e., *Tubastrea* coral, *Dendronephthya* soft coral, need to be fed, the nutritional requirements of photosynthetic Cnidarians is easily exceeded if they are properly illuminated in a reef tank. Keep in mind that they can derive quite a great amount of nutrition from detritus borne bacteria, as well as the bacteria which grow and thrive on the rich carbohydrate media of the Cnidarian's mucous coat. Many corals and anemones are continuously "reeling" this mucous trap in using ciliary currents to harvest their prey — and you haven't even been able to see this! In my experience, and I'm not alone in this observation, extra food is only pollution that can harm your anemones. If they occasionally catch a piece of food dropped by a fish, it is no cause for concern, but I would not go out of my way to feed them. I have witnessed anemones outgrown aquariums when kept "unfed," and I have observed so many shrivel up when their overzealous owners fed them too much.

Q. Dear Mr. Dewey — you hooked me with George Smit's excellent minireef series. In spite of my excitement, I decided to wait. My thinking was, a couple of years would identify and resolve possible problems with this advanced technology. In my opinion, however, just the opposite has happened and now I'm totally confused. Let me give you an example . . .

Dr. Blok discussed the need to retain CO_2 by partially closing the cover holes and substituting inert gravel for coral gravel in the wet filter.

Albert Thiel recommends we fertilize our system with chelated iron supplements and CO_2 using an expensive reactor/injector.

Julian Sprung believes that neither CO_2 enhancement nor iron supplements are the solution, suggesting further that the wet filter should be a foam block acting as a second prefilter.

George Smit disagrees, recommending that we use calcite in the wet filter to lower CO_2 levels, increase hardness and buffer the system.

Each author has absolutely perfect pictures to prove their points. Since each is also a representative of their own commercial products and, therefore, competitors, I expect some bias. But what I see is a total lack of agreement on even the basic principles of system needs or design.

The problem is it's expensive just to get started, let alone finding out that I did it wrong and have to spend more to correct my mistakes. If the experts disagree, how does the hobbyist determine what's right or wrong? Bob Frishman, Huntington Beach, California

A. As can be seen from the salutation, Mr. Frishman did not address this letter to me, but I will attempt to answer it.

I will use this opportunity to explain the reasoning behind these different viewpoints, the positive aspects and disadvantages, and the reasoning for my own particular point of view. In doing this I will, of necessary, step on a few toes. I'll try to walk gently.

Let's start out with George Smit since he can be congratulated for opening the eyes of aquarists in this country and producing a surge of interest that has had a tremendous effect on the aquarium industry, resulting in the development here of newer and better technologies than Smit originally presented. Mr. Smit recommends using calcite in the wet filter for the purpose of buffering. This advice stems from an old notion that carbonate materials were needed in seawater aquariums in order to stabilize pH. Research has shown, on the contrary, that carbonate gravel does not dissolve and buffer the water, but that they actually pull part of the water's natural buffer out of the solution. Calcium bicarbonate, an important part of the buffering system of seawater, will precipitate on calcite (calcium carbonate). If you would like to read more about this I suggest you contact Mr. Tom Frakes of Aquarium Systems, Inc. and ask for back issues of SeaScope dealing with buffering media and pH. In fact, while Smit describes the carbonate/bicarbonate buffering system according to Spotte, if you read Spotte's books you will find references to the inability of carbonate media to buffer to pH 8.3.

"Okay, Julian," you say, "so I don't want calcite!"
"Hold on a minute," I say, "there's a lot more to know."

It is interesting to note that with the recognition of the modified natural system of Dr. Jean Jaubert (see appendix) we have come full circle in a way, back to using calcareous gravel. But the gravel does not have water flowing through it, so it does not become a dirt trap.

In time, the negative effect on pH diminishes as the surface of the gravel becomes polluted and, yes, you can have a successful aquarium using calcite as Smit's photos indicate. Your success will be limited, however. The fact that _Caulerpa_ grows so well in Smit's system is indicative of a high nutrient situation, something that is detrimental to scleractinian (hard) corals. True coral reefs do not look like his tanks. Smit's aquaria appear more like bay environments — which is not bad if that's what you're trying to duplicate. His aquaria are beautiful.

Important rule: Success is relative, or beauty is in the eye of the beholder. Corollary to the above rule: Knowledge and experience affect one's taste.

Smit began his first series in this magazine asking aquarists if was time for a change. I liked this attitude. Still, in my opinion, the persistent advice to place gravel — of any kind — in the wet section of the filter merely shows an unwillingness to let go of the old undergravel filter. It is an undergravel filter placed outside of the aquarium, with most of the same disadvantages. In time it will clog with bacterial slime and detritus that perpetually rains down from the dry section. It will need to be cleaned, and this is a chore. Also, being submerged, it creates a huge oxygen demand on the system — not what we

Note: **I no longer recommend continuous use of mechanical filters in the sump or elsewhere in the system.**

want in theory a least. You should be able to understand now why Sea Kleer Reefs, Inc. uses a foam cartridge. It traps the dirt to prevent pump clogging, is easy to service, and is small so that it does not use up much oxygen, this all being aside from the fact that it is inert. The sponge is not intended to be used for denitrification. Important rule #2: The easier a system is to service, the more likely the aquarist is to take care of it.

Let's backtrack a moment for those who are wondering why I'm so dead set against gravel and sand considering these substrates are definitely an important component of the reef environment. There is a difference between aquarium substrates and reef substrates. The difference is that the sand on the reef is clean. It is as if someone were pouring bleach over it all the time. The way this works is not a matter of dilution by the volume of water, and the effect cannot be duplicated in the aquarium by gravel washing. Rather it is a product of the motion of the water — the physical parameter of surge producing a gentle to and fro motion which has the effect of one giant broom sweeping the detritus up off the bottom from amongst the sand grains, into the water column or, in observable rows, toward the shore, lagoon, or grassbed. The shifting of the individual sand grains not only frees the sediment of suspendable material, but it has a further cleansing function in that the grains grind against each other, polishing off precipitated nutrients (which only accumulate in the gravel in an aquarium, as Smit noted), and algae. In my opinion, because of this flow of water, the reef is in a position where it is mostly exporting and cleaning itself, despite the tight recycling and conversion of carbon and phosphorus. In a closed system aquarium, just the opposite is true. Sediments are excellent nutrient traps, which is fortunate for the reef but, in the aquarium, without the control of powerful surge, nutrients accumulate rapidly and create undesirable effects (i.e., problem algae, coral death).

On another subject, at last, Thiel's recommendations about CO_2 and iron fertilization stem from techniques developed by Kaspar Horst and Horst Kipper of Dupla Aquaristik for the optimization of freshwater planted aquaria. While these techniques, which are beautifully

My opinion has changed on these subjects too. Carbon dioxide is useful in conjunction with a pH controller to keep the pH from climbing too high and to supply CO_2 to the aquarium during the day when photosynthesis can deplete it. Iron does have some observable benefit to corals, though it can also stimulate algae growth.

*Gee, that was not quite accurate. CO_2 can temporarily depress pH, but it can also raise alkalinity since it forms carbonate (CO_3^{-2}) and bicarbonate ions (HCO_3^-) readily when dissolved in seawater. Calcium reactors using CO_2 have recently gained in popularity as a means of adding calcium to reef aquaria. It remains to be seen how the results compare with the use of kalkwasser. Nilsen and Brockman present a comparative review in *Aquarium Frontiers* journal, (in press).

explained and demonstrated in *The Optimum Aquarium* by K. Horst and H. Kipper, are the ultimate for freshwater planted aquaria, their use and benefit is limited in marine reef set ups. Basically, what I advise those interested in such systems is that they work beautifully if your ultimate goal is to grow plants. I see no benefit to the coral — zooxanthellae obtain CO_2 from the coral's respiration, and I have not yet witnessed any benefit to the corals from the addition of iron. I do not want to create the impression that zooxanthellae do not use iron, rather, I believe there is no shortage of iron available to them. This is only my opinion.

As a point of interest, there are reactors in which CO_2 is bubbled over a carbonate media to liberate calcium carbonate. This works, unlike Smit's suggestion. Still, as you might expect, I believe the need for such reactors is small in a reef aquarium — unless you are also fertilizing with CO_2, since it (the CO_2) lowers the carbonate hardness of the water.* This is why Thiel advocates exceptionally high values for carbonate hardness, in opposition to nature where hardness is typically about 8 dkh.

Now to the grand finale in this answer. The fact that my logic is logical doesn't mean a thing. What really counts is what happens when we apply it in practice. Ultimately, your experience tells what works best for you — with this experience you develop the "witchcraft: — the art that transcends the rules and recipes of any aquarist. It is time for you to get started experiencing, not just reading. Theory is great for armchair aquarists, bur real aquarists know how to suffer! Finally, you should remember, above all, that I am right, of course! Good luck, and I hope you can accept my words with the seriousness and the humor in which they were intended.

Ah, wonderful! We are done with the questions, so now we can discuss what you've been waiting a whole month to read: How to catch those darned mantis shrimp.

Several methods exist for capturing these beasts but, unfortunately, none are really easy or foolproof. Starting with the simplest technique, the aquarist may observe a mantis shrimp enter a particular rock and just remove that rock from the tank. This is all fine and dandy if the

*They are now available commercially, ask your dealer.

rock isn't supporting the whole creation. Considering this, many aquarists have devised traps for mantis shrimp.* The fish trap I discussed last month could work, but the jar would have to be fairly long as these guys are both smart and fast. A better trap was described recently in the Windows to the Sea Club newsletter. Therein was a reprint of an article from the Marine Aquarium Society of Victoria, written by Andrew Walker. Mr. Walker placed an elastic band around a small plastic hinged box, baited it with a piece of fish impaled on a matchstick, and propped the box open with this matchstick — not too complicated a trap for all you "Wile E. Coyotes" out there, and it worked, for Mr. Walker at least. I had thought of a trap that incorporated a glow stick in an acrylic box, as is used by scientists attempting to trap deep water crustaceans, but was informed by Dr. Roy Caldwell at the University of California at Berkeley, that this wouldn't work for the stomatopods that we have in our aquaria. Dr. Caldwell has been studying these guys for twenty years and has come to accept their ability to evade capture. In fact he is interested in their behavior and their remarkable intelligence. He warned that if you miss once, a mantis shrimp will be so much wiser the next time. I had tried ridding rock of mantis shrimp in a bucket by bubbling CO_2 for a while and found that it drove some out and actually killed them without harming the rock. Dr. Caldwell said that he had tried this too, among other things, and found that there were still plenty of mantis shrimp that could survive deep within the rock. What was his suggestion? Use a "Borneo prawn snare" or employ an octopus. Considering the risk to fishes, an octopus is probably not practical for most aquarists. Dr. Caldwell makes his trap by creating a noose out of the wire from a twist tie and affixing it to a coat hanger. The noose is stuffed down into the hole that a mantis shrimp has just retreated into, and a piece of bait is placed in front of the hole. If you push the noose deep enough into the hole, as soon as you see his head emerge, says Dr. Caldwell, you can pull up on the hanger to snare him. Can you see yourself doing this? I bet you can.

July 1989

Last month we talked a little more about live rock, so why not continue the trend? It has come to the attention of hobbyists and pet dealers that live rock shipments have been halted in Florida pending evaluation of the industry and its collection practices to determine the means, if allowable, of regulation to protect Florida's reef and hardbottom areas. Similarly, Hawaiian collectors have observed signs along their coasts warning them not to remove rock or rubble from the shore or reef. What next? Let's all hope that government officials decide that regulation of rock collecting is possible, and that collectors abide by the laws established to protect nature and their own business. As I explained in a previous column, removal of loose rubble from hardbottom areas, when accompanied by equivalent replenishment with suitable materials, is a safe practice.

I have been asked by many hobbyists whether there is a preference for reverse osmosis, deionized, or distilled water to be used for water make-up or mixing up of salt.* At Sea Kleer Reefs we are using water that is pre-filtered mechanically and with activated carbon, then reverse osmosis filtered and passed through cationic and anionic ion-exchange columns for post-filtration. The end result is some very pure water! Judging by the very slow exhaustion of the deionizing resin beads, it is apparent that the reverse osmosis filter does the largest job. A number of hobbyists have taken my suggestion and have purchased reverse osmosis filters only. Most have reported dramatic reduction in the growth of algae on the glass, and reduction or elimination of "hair algae," though some aquarists report that these beasts continue to grow. It is hard to evaluate the reason why one experience differs from another, though I believe that a number of factors are involved. The first is the availability of nutrients stored in the substrate or rocks. This may vary depending on the amount of time nutrient inputs (water, foods, trace additives, etc.), the amount of substrate, and even the type of substrate. Differences in the fauna on the live rock also play a role, as the organisms are intimately involved in the exchange of nutrients between water and substrate. Finally, herbivores can really help get things under control, especially when combined with good prefilter maintenance, as their waste can be

*Purification processes generally remove 95% of impurities. If the impurity is of high concentration, the remaining 5% left in the water can be significant. If two stages are used, i.e. R.O. and D.I., then theoretically 95% is removed of the remaining 5% from the first stage. Sometimes tap or well water is not contaminated with phosphate, nitrate, heavy metals, or pesticides, and it can be rich in calcium and trace elements. Under these circumstances it can be used unfiltered.

trapped and removed, thus exporting nutrients from the system. Herbivore feces are often "pelletized" and can be observed trapped in the prefilter. These fecal pellets play an important role on the reef in nature since there, too, they are exported by currents and, to some extent, also trapped and eaten by many reef inhabitants including fish and corals.

I no longer recommend angelfish as they are persistent pests of fleshy corals, some soft corals, and tridacnid clams. However, in a reef tank lacking these, (i.e. with small polyped stony corals only) the angels will do little harm. *Ctenochaetus* sp. tangs are very prone to *Amyloodinium* "velvet" disease and so I don't recommend them anymore. *Zebrasoma* sp. tangs are better. Small hermit crabs are also great herbivores, see appendix.

Some good fish herbivores for a closed system reef tank include: Chevron tang, Kole tang, Flameback Pygmy angel, Resplendent angel, Atlantic Pygmy angel, and the Atlantic Red-lipped blenny. Other tanks or surgeonfish are also excellent herbivores, but depending on their name (i.e., Fred, Martha, Sam, etc) they may or may not be angelic in the coral garden! Some blennies mistake polyps for algae, and may actually help spread certain soft corals by nipping off polyps and spitting them out.

Personally, I like invertebrate herbivores, especially molluscan ones. Some good invertebrate herbivores include: *Diadema* urchins, small short-spined urchins, limpets, chitons, certain "top shells" such as *Turbo* sp., *Astraea tectum,* some *Calliostoma* sp., and *Trochus* sp., and some other snails including *Nerita* sp. which have a habit of crawling out of the tank, and *Cerithium* sp. All of the above are bulldozers to some extent, so it is best to choose small specimens. Although they are beautiful, I don't like urchins for small tanks because they may strip the rock of its coralline algae. In large aquaria the coralline algae grow in pace with urchin grazing and can be assisted by them. The rasping by fish and invertebrate herbivores, in fact, is an important means of dispersal for coralline algae. Limpets, as I have been told and recently observed, can develop a taste for mushroom anemones as well as encrusting soft corals. They will not systematically destroy a colony, but, rather, they just take a bite now and them. I watched a couple of limpets strip away the lovely growth of green star polyp that I had proudly displaced growing on the front glass of my aquarium. They didn't bother the main colony nor its growth on the bottom of the aquarium. They only ate what was on the front glass, and continue to do this whenever the star polyp grows up on the glass. Ah well, I love 'em anyway!

Some aquarists employ crabs as herbivores. I don't like crabs very much because most grow too large and develop a taste for one's most cherished fish. Sally Lightfoot crabs are cute and beautiful, appearing like a little flat drummer as they graze, but they soon become big and ugly. Mithrax crabs, aka "hardback" or "coral crabs" are excellent herbivores that will polish a rock as well as any snail, but most species grow too large and may eat coral polyps. There is, however, a diminutive species from the Atlantic which is similar to the common shiny green *Mithrax sculptus*, but which is cream colored with olive colored claws, and a few wine colored blotches on the back in the smallest specimens. I think it may be an undescribed species, and it happens to be a good long-term herbivore in a reef tank.

Finally, one fair warning: not all snails and "slugs" are herbivorous. For instance, the egg cowrie (white, just like an egg) will eat your *Sarcophyton* leather coral. Cowries make interesting pets by themselves, but are really slimy beasts, and not desirable in a reef tank. Wentletrap snails will devour your orange *Tubastrea* coral. Flamingo tongues are murder on gorgonians. Nudibranchs, in addition, are mostly carnivores, preying usually on specific hydroids, sponges, anemones, or bryozoans. The nudibranch-like anaspid, *Aplysia* (sea hare) is a good herbivore, though bulky and messy as well as having the most undesirable habit of releasing a mildly toxic purple dye in the water. *Tridachea crispata* is another herbivorous nudibranch-like slug (Sacoglossan) which is very beautiful but, unfortunately, tends to go over the overflow.

And now for everyone's favorite part of the show . . .

Q. My 30 gallon aquarium has been in operation for about two years using the old undergravel system. After reading about the reef systems in FAMA, I converted over to it around 9 months ago with Actinic lighting and an Ocean Reef Micro-Reef add-on unit powered by a Fluval 202 containing Chemi-Pure™ and Poly Filter™.

The tank contains one skunk clown which I've had over a year, a small yellow tang which keeps unwanted filamentous algae in check, along with a small brown sea urchin.

I also have a healthy coral banded shrimp, an Atlantic anemone that has just reproduced, and a lush growth of *Caulerpa*. Ammonia, nitrite, and nitrate are all zero!

Under these conditions, why can't I just try some live coral without having to increase the bioload with a tank full of live rock? Previous articles in FAMA imply that this live rock is an absolute necessity, but are vague as to the reasons why. Please explain. Brian Ciske, Milwaukee, Wisconsin

A. Your question is very apropos this month, Brian, as we may no longer have a choice to make in this regard! Last month I explained why I think live rock, and the source, or type, of live rock can make a difference. Now I'd like to develop my explanation further by including a little philosophical perspective. Basically one has to look at one's tank objectively and decide just what kind of aquarium it will be. It is true that with the proper physical and chemical parameters met, one can maintain individual species in any aquarium, indefinitely. "Success," therefore, can be defined on many levels. One can have a successful fish tank, or invertebrate tank, as you do, Brian, but a captive reef system is a different sort of creation. I guess the confusion lies in the suggestion made by many "reef converts" that corals and other delicate invertebrates can only be maintained in the new reef tanks, and that such tanks have to have so many pounds per gallon (a ridiculous assertion considering the variation in rock density) because so and so said so — so there! Truthfully, many of the organisms now maintained in reef tanks can be maintained in simpler, "old" systems. There are still numerous organisms which are extremely difficult to maintain even now in any system. Now, I don't wish to imply that a complex reef ecosystem can be created using the old filtration technology, but I have seen and have established some beautiful invertebrate displays with live coral, anemones, sponges and algae in aquaria with not much more than an undergravel filter. These tanks keep the reef life healthy, and actually are as beautiful and heavily stocked as most of the wet/dry filtered tanks I have seen, but they are not reef ecosystems.

There are different schools of thought in this regard and,

truly, the definition might seem fuzzy when one compares one successful tank to another, but experience brings an appreciation of the limits of each closed system technique. Yes, having more live rock does make a better ecosystem, as I explained last month. Yes, there is a big difference made by the newer filtration techniques for both fresh and saltwater. But, no, there is no single exclusive road to a successful aquarium. You decide ultimately what your ideal tank is. By the way, live rock does not increase bioload, really. Initially, when it is fouling, of course, it does, but aside from oxygen consumption at night, the rocks do not stress the water. In fact, they filter it.

Q. Regarding your comment on the use of gravel in the wet portion of the trickle filter, what would you say to George Smit's insistence on the benefits of calcite, both in stabilization of pH and the water quality?

Can you also comment on quarantine of invertebrates and live rock? I subscribe to a lot of marine fish magazines, and no one has really written anything on this topic. I fail to understand this. We all emphasize proper quarantine of fish to prevent wipeouts and loss of fish, but the impression I get about live rock and invertebrates is buy them and put them straight into the display tank. Don't they carry disease and parasites, too?
Yours sincerely, Dr. Lim Kok Hoo, Johore, Malaysia

A. To answer your first question:
(1) Re-read last month's column.
(2) Re-read the answer to the previous question.

As for your second question, I have been asked about quarantine of invertebrates many times. I remember years ago when I would show other aquarists my tanks, how some would shake their heads asking about all those awful bugs that come in the aquarium with live rock. Upon further inquiry I usually discovered that these folks didn't worry about quarantining fish because the "knew how to pick a disease-free fish," But live food or inverts sent them running for the medicine cabinet. I guess there is no need to go into a long lecture on the fact that there is no such thing as a disease-free fish, and

I don't mean to imply that you didn't realize this. It is true that some fish parasites can be introduced with invertebrates and live rock, but compared to the risk of adding an un-quarantined fish, the chances of a problem are very slim. I do not quarantine invertebrates and don't recommend doing so. Please do re-read last month's column where I discuss "seeding" live rock. I guess this is a form of quarantine I am recommending, though disease is not the concern. I have been feeding my fish fresh seaweed, crustaceans, and clams from the ocean and bay for years and have never encountered a disease as a result. But the addition of a new fish has created problems time and time again.

I'd like to close this month's column with a letter I found very amusing.

Dear Mr. Sprung:

Some time early in 1988 my daughter brought home a scrawny goldfish inside a cloudy plastic bowl, and then she promptly left it in the kitchen and forgot about it. I don't like fish, so I attempted ignoring it. A few days passed, I, casually, feeding it lumps of flake food. About the fifth day I gave the fish a name, "Cutie." My first mistake. One day I notice Cutie was swaying in a funny way, so I called a pet store and they suggested I was overfeeding it. Cutie died and I couldn't sleep all night. Next day I washed the gravel and bought two new Cuties and a small pump and filter ($.$.$). Weeks went by bringing the cycle of 100% mortality rate and repurchase, etc., and to me a sense of failure and yet determination to succeed in the face of such defeats. I made the rounds of all the pet stores in a 20 mile radius, keeping in mind that I don't really care for fish . . . and I asked every pet store owner where I was going wrong, since I didn't think I was overfeeding.

Casual observation would lead you to believe my kitchen was now a biology lab — test tubes on each finger, balancing 6 drops here, 7 there, and 8 in the other. Finally after months of night vigils, talking to my fish and feeding them with no success, I made the decision to change my well water to bottled water and voila! My fish stretched out their fins and decided to stay! Now I have Onyx, Romulus, Apple Too, and Boy-Boy — fancy and happy goldfish! My question is (I'm not really interested, of course) but what is a reef system? I've read from every magazine and book on fish, bits and pieces about facets of the reef system, but I don't understand the ABC's of this method, except how to spell it. I know that I have an extreme interest in the fish that live in the reef, with anemones and corals, etc. How can I find out fully what I'm embarking on? I treasure my sleep. Thank you, Kristine Sullivan

A. Thank you, Kris. Just keep on reading this column if you feel like it. What more can I say?

I have just found the best identification guide for marine algae, *Marine Plants of the Caribbean, a field guide from Florida to Brazil*, by Diane Littler, Mark M. Littler, Katina E. Bucher, and James N. Norris. It is published by the Smithsonian Institution Press. This book is a must for reef keeping hobbyists. For the first time identification is made simple because all the species are shown in excellent color photographs. The book also includes information on plant life histories, classification, habitats, nomenclature, and even tips on underwater photography! I am ecstatic about this book — could you tell?

See you next time.

September 1989

A number of you have asked me about how organisms should be arranged with respect to water flow, so this month, we begin with the subject of orientation on the reef.

The particular mode of growth and the ultimate shape or form of a sessile organism in the marine environment is the product of several possible factors (light, substrate, neighbors, commensals, food source, for instance), but water motion has perhaps the most powerful influence on organism shape. As aquarists, we generally build our reefs with "preformed" animals, ones which have grown to make the best use of the environment in which they occurred. If we do not closely match the physical parameters of the water flow which sculpted them (i.e., direction, velocity, turbulence, surge), then they will grow in a new orientation, die, or a combination of both.

While any of a variety of marine animals and plants could be used to demonstrate such orientation to water flow, I will limit discussion to sponges and gorgonians, since I have studied them carefully both in the field and in my aquaria.

Sponges, as I explained in a previous column, have very specific requirements for water flow because of the high oxygen demand of both them and their commensals, the need to obtain food, and the need to remove the metabolic wastes of both them and their commensals. Although sponges have flagellated "collar cells" lining the channels within them, the currents these little whippers generate are greatly assisted by the flow of water past the sponge. Such assistance becomes more critical as sponges become larger and more complex.

The growth of finger-like sponges tends to be parallel with the direction of water flow when tidal currents are the major shaping force. Given some surge (to-and-fro) motion, finger-like sponges tend to grow straight up, with oscula randomly located around branches. Encrusting finger-like sponges grow parallel with the direction of the most powerful flow (surge or current) and have oscula only on the upper surface. Such a sponge growing on a vertical wall where surge might produce an up and down motion will grow up toward the surface and with oscula only on the exposed side. Rounded sponges can take currents from any direction, and will adapt to your errors in placement, but look at the pattern of oscula on them and you can find a parallel which indicates their original orientation. Oblongation and raised surface features often offer clues as well. Some sponges, the lovely blue species from Indonesia, for instance, have the oscula located at the tips of cone-like projections. When I place one of these sponges, I look for a site where the water will well upwards through the grooves between the projecting oscula so that an even, strong, flow is going from bottom to top. This flow generates the kind of pressure drop at the oscula (by Bernoulli's principal) that these sponges like. Small pieces of most sponges can be placed most anywhere with success because of their small density. Most small pieces will begin to encrust a rock until they "find" a suitable location to project off the substrate into the current.

Most of the live rock we use is thoroughly riddled with a boring sponge called *Cliona*. It often dies in shipping, which contributes greatly to the fouling initially encountered. Strong currents and surge ensure that this sponge gets the oxygen it needs.

Gorgonians are wonderful creatures for the reef aquarium, and most are easy to keep when properly oriented. Orientation by gorgonians can be divided into two categories since there are photosynthetic ones and non-photosynthetic ones. (Some sponges, as I explained in a previous column, are also photosynthetic, and their form is at least partly due to the need to gather light.) The influence of light on those gorgonians which are photosynthetic is to make them grow up toward the surface, much the same as in plants. The effect of water movement is more dramatic, and is essentially the same for photosynthetic and non-photosynthetic ones.

I became interested in gorgonian orientation after noticing a contradiction between what I read in text books and what I saw when diving. Many texts are quick to point out that fan-like gorgonians grow in such a way that they are perpendicular to the current flow. Their reasoning is that such growth makes them effective "nets" for the plankton which they eat. This all seemed fine to me, except that the fans and other gorgonians I saw growing off the coast of Florida all grew parallel with the current! In fact, a diver could simply scan down a patch of them on the hardbottom and observe how neatly they all lined up. I knew right away that it was not current that they oriented perpendicular to, but surge. Even in the bushy gorgonians I could see that the long axis of their base was perpendicular to surge. I had it all figured out, I thought, and proudly told my professors that the books were wrong! I was certain that gorgonians oriented parallel with the flow of tidal currents, that the current and surge directions would always be perpendicular to each other. I reasoned that the orientation to surge allowed them to flap back and forth, exposing more polyps and surface to the light. I had also noticed the same type of orientation in an alga, *Udotea*, along the shore. I reasoned that the flapping combined with the current flow offered an even better arrangement for food capture than given in the texts. Also it was apparent that this flapping assisted the shedding process gorgonians use to get rid of epiphytes. Some of my reasoning was correct, but I was temporarily baffled one evening in the dry Tortugas when I realized that *Gorgonia ventalina* growing along a sea wall there were definitely oriented perpendicular to the current flow. I was depressed. This hypothesis was no longer sound. The next day, however, when the glass-smooth calm of the previous evening changed to a light afternoon chop, my spirits were lifted. I had assumed that the waves would behave the same here as they did along the Florida coast, approaching parallel to the shore. They didn't. The wave surge was clearly perpendicular to the orientation of the fans, actually flowing in parallel with the tidal current. A little modification of the hypothesis was all that was necessary. Gorgonians, in fact, oriented perpendicular to the stronger water flow, which was usually surge. In deep water, non-photosynthetic gorgonians experience little or no surge — the texts were right about their orientation. Some months later, while doing some research in the library I came across some references on the subject of sea fan orientation. All "my" hypotheses had been worked out long before I had even seen a gorgonian. This long story surely has a purpose, but in retrospect, I don't know why I'm telling you about this.

Many of the gorgonians we keep are candelabrum shaped or at least they grown in one plane. These should be placed in an aquarium in concordance with my slightly mistaken first hypothesis, that is, place them parallel with the current from your pump or powerhead. You will notice that the current flowing across their branches will cause them to rock perpendicular to the current, and this will make them happy. Nifty!

One final note of interest. In the study of sea fans, a researcher sectioned the bases of numerous fans and discovered that they were twisted. It was apparent that the fans did not settle in the proper orientation, but that they had gradually changed their orientation. In the aquarium gorgonians often develop kinks that indicate a correction via growth toward the light and with respect to current.

I just can't bear to write a column without talking about nutrients in the aquarium, and I hope you'll bear with me while I explain an analogy I came up with while driving and fiddling with the radio. If you think of your aquarium as being like a stereo system (pay attention now, I'm not kidding), nutrients can be equated with the power (on/off) button, lighting with the volume dial, and algae growth with loudness of sound. When the power is "on," if you increase the volume dial, the sound will become louder. Likewise, in the presence of nutrients, the more light (intensity) you provide, the more algae will grow. Conversely, if the power button is "off," the volume dial may be turned "all the way" and no sound will be emitted by the speakers. It follows then that with no nutrients present, lighting can be increased without a proportional increase in algae growth. The algae will not grow at all if the limit, "no nutrients" is reached. It is nice to analyze things like this in the theoretical sense because sometimes their nature is more apparent when carried to extremes. Of course, in a closed system it is impossible to achieve "no nutrients," and a lighting increase will bring about a proportional increase in the algae growth. However, limiting available nutrients does reduce the magnitude of the proportional increase. Therefore, reducing all potential nutrient sources (i.e., make-up water, detritus), will have noticeable affects on algal growth.

Interestingly, another factor affects the potential algal growth in an aquarium, and that is the presence of algae! Carried to extremes again, of course a sterile aquarium, even with nutrients, will not grow algae. While this may seem obvious, there is more to the presence of algae effect and its affect on algal growth. Not only do you need algae to grow more algae, but also the more algae you have, the more algae will grow. This "snowball" effect is what makes hair algae problems so devastating. There are three principal causes for this effect. First is that more algal mass will release more spores and gametes which, given enough nutrients, will continue to grow. Second is that algal mass itself is nutrient rich or, put another way, algal mass is a potential source of nutrients. Third is the sneaky ability of algae, by virtue of their design, to trap detritus, which is another potential nutrient source. Algae accomplish this by slowing the velocity of water flowing over them, a trick which makes detritus fall out on them. Dense algae and ones with a surrounding growth of fuzzy filaments trap detritus like mechanical filters.

Just one more notion to drive the point home and enlighten the aquarist. I just explained that algal mass is a potential nutrient source. Therein lies part of the explanation for the reef's mysterious ability to live in nutrient poor water. In an aquarium full of algae, for instance, a test for ammonia will read "zero," and a test for orthophosphate will probably also read zero, or nearly at least. Bacterial decomposition of the plant tissue liberates usable nitrogen and phosphorus for additional plant growth, and nutrients added by the aquarist are rapidly incorporated into the plants. Thus an aquarium full of algae, and an aquarium with no algae can have very similar nutrient levels in the water. If we could "boil these tanks down," however, we could see the difference. The nutrients are not so much in the water as they are stored as a potential nutrient source, in rock, detritus, and the living plants. How can we tell, then, what the true level of nutrient availability is? Well, truthfully there are differences measurable in the water, though often subtle, but interestingly the algae themselves are good indicators of nutrient availability, not so much in their rate of growth or mass, but actually in the concentration of nutrients stored in their tissue! The quantity of nitrogen and phosphorus stored in the tissue of a plant actually varies with the availability of these nutrients (Lapointe, Littler, and Littler, 1987). This is at least part of the reason why the suggested "R.O. treatment" takes a long time to have an effect for some aquaria, when for others the effect is immediate.

While on the subject, I thought you might find it interesting that the animals we employ to keep the algae under control actually are, themselves, zones of elevated nutrient potential that tend to increase the growth of the turfs they feed on. A recent study showed that nitrogen-limited reef

Of course other outputs include protein skimming and the use of activated carbon. When natural denitrification in the system is able to maintain low nitrate levels, then food inputs are important to maintain coral growth. The same is true if algal turf filtration is stripping ammonia and nitrate from the water...with little food input the corals will eventually starve. Furthermore, algal turf filters, protein skimmers, and chemical filtration remove trace elements which must be replenished.

*Please look up the subject Kalkwasser in appendix and in *The Reef Aquarium, Vol 1.*

algal turfs exhibited much higher rates of productivity when grazed by sea urchins. The turfs were enhanced by the ammonia excretions. (Williams and Carpenter, 1988.)

So we see now that nutrient levels in an aquarium are not merely a water quality, but actually a whole system quality. With this idea in mind it should be clearer why I recommend being conservative with system inputs (food, make-up water) and liberal with system outputs (water changes, detritus removal, prefilter cleaning, and algal turf filtration).

It's a pretty safe bet that I'll have more to say in future columns about nutrient potential and flux in the marine environment. It's one of my favorite topics, could you tell?

Q. A part of my company's manufacturing process requires water to be as pure as possible. Tap water is distilled, then filtered down to the angstrom level. All elements, chemicals, and impurities are removed. Various testing procedures show it to be 99.999% pure. Can I use this water in an established mini-reef system? With all of the chemicals, elements, and other hazards removed, is it too pure to use? Would I have to doctor it up to make it usable? Terry Brandt, Costa Mesa, CA

A. Of course if all elements were removed, you would have no water, but I know what you mean and if the water is as pure as you say, by all means use it! No, you would not have to doctor it up. In theory it might seem that such water would lower your pH and carbonate hardness. In practice (at Sea Kleer Reefs, Inc., and many customers' tanks) this does not happen. One word of caution: The water you describe is very aggressive so that storage vessels must be inert and exposure to air must be avoided to maintain the pure integrity of the water.*

Continuing right along with the watery theme.

Q. What can you tell me about the use of natural sea water in an aquarium? I'm concerned that it might bring in parasites that make my fish or invertebrates sick. George Kopit, Palm Beach, Florida

It is possible to introduce disease causing organisms with fresh seawater, as I observed working with open system aquariums at a fish hatchery. Still, I have never witnessed disease occur as a result of a single water change with fresh natural seawater (as opposed to the continuous exchange in open systems, a situation that both flushes out parasites and introduces them). In my experience, when trace element supplementation is a part of routine maintenance, artificial seawater affords results exactly equal to natural seawater. Of course impurities in the freshwater used also affect the results. The only reason to use natural seawater is because it may be cheaper if you have it in your backyard.

A. Imagine my thoughts the day a customer from Florida called me and said that his store's marine expert had told him that artificial water was better than real sea water. (Where's a lighting bolt when you really need one?) As long as the water you collect is not in the vicinity of sewage disposal, which might generate elevated levels of harmful bacteria, there is no risk of parasite introduction. As I've said before, the greatest risk of parasite introduction occurs with the addition of fish to the system. There are a couple of important rules regarding the use of natural sea water. It is not necessary to filter the water before putting it in your aquarium, but it is not harmful to do so either. If you do not filter the water (I don't), then it must be used immediately, within several hours, or then only after two weeks storage in the dark. This is owing to the rapid dying off and fouling by zooplankton and phytoplankton which can make the water downright toxic 24 hours after collection if you let it sit without circulation. Aeration can extend the life of the plankton so you are encouraged to do so. A couple of weeks in the dark allows the dead bacteria to decompose and settle. The water can then be used or stored indefinitely. As indicated, I prefer to use the water immediately. The best place to collect water is far offshore, by boat, but one can find excellent water on shore especially on incoming tide at inlets. Palm Beach has some of the clearest and cleanest water in the continental U.S. When I lived in Florida I often collected my water there.

Q. Several times in aquarium stores I have seen carpet anemones with vibrantly colored blue, yellow, or pink bases and/or tentacles. There is some confusion about whether these colors are natural, or are the result of injected "dyes." Are there such things as dyed anemones, and if they are, is the dye harmful to the anemone? Gregory C. Peterson, Chicago, Illinois

A. Well, considering those tacky painted freshwater glassfish, I can understand your concern, especially when exceptionally colored marine invertebrates tend to command a very high price. In general, most of the brilliantly colored anemones you see are not dyed. Incredible, aren't they? What may lead you to believe that they are dyed is that these colors are pigments which develop under specific lighting regimes in nature, and in our aquaria the differences in lighting can cause the anemones to fade or take on additional colors that subdue the brilliant ones. White carpet anemones with colorful tentacles and bases tend to take on a rich brown color, while keeping the blue, green, pink, or purple, when placed in an aquarium. This is because of the size and density of the photosynthetic pigment units increases to be more efficient at using the available light intensity which is lower in an aquarium than in nature. I recall a science project by a friend of mine in Miami, Jean Turner, who dyed Atlantic *Condylactis* anemones. Placed in a dish of dyed water, they would take up some of the water and, in turn, some of the color. I do not know how long this stain lasted, but it appeared to be nontoxic. I don't think the suppliers or collectors are trying to fool us, but there is the possibility that it can be done, especially around Easter time.

Note: I have occasionally seen *Heteractis* sp. and *Condylactis* anemones offered for sale which appeared to have been dyed yellow. Naturally green pigmented anemones that have "bleached" (lost pigment) often are bright yellow.

Well that does it for this month.

References
Lapointe, B.E., M.M. Littler, and D.S. Littler: A comparison of nutrient-limited productivity in macroalgae from a Caribbean barrier reef and from a mangrove ecosystem. *Aquatic Botany*, 28, 243-255 (1987).

Williams, S.L. and R.C. Carpenter: Nitrogen-limited primary productivity of coral reef algal turfs: potential contribution of ammonium excreted by *Diadema antillarum. Mar. Ecol. Prog. Ser.*, 47, 145-152 (1988).

October 1989

Last month we discussed some analogies and, for the sake of maintaining a sort of unified continuum of thought, I thought I'd offer another. Here's an analogy which can be employed in the explanation of a number of processes, including at least the limitation of U.V. sterilization and the reason for the success of the reef in the desert of the sea.

Imagine a room with a perpetual but controlled fire in the middle of it that produces copious amounts of smoke. Now also imagine that someone has installed a sort of air filter on this room, and it is capable of filtering the volume of the room in excess of ten times per hour, returning air to the room, that is completely free of smoke. (To those of you craving more quantitative data, bothered by my qualitative definition of "copious smoke," I say, "Too bad, this is my analogy!") One can see that in such a room there will always be smoke (yes, until the fire runs out, but I said the fire was perpetual, the fuel is given) and, likewise, in such a system there will always be parasites in the aquarium, or bacteria and other plankton on the reef. Naturally, this also applies to food availability in the reef aquarium, though the analogy is really correct only for bacteria and detritus, zooplankton production not being copious.

Moving right along now to something completely different, the subject of how to cycle a tank is yet another one full of opinions designed by the experts to confound the beginning hobbyist, or at least to generate controversy and intrigue about which opposing viewpoint is best. I'm not going to single out a "best" technique, but I will present some alternatives for different situations.

As we all know, an aquarium must first be "cycled," conditioned, established, seasoned, run-in, etc., in order to support a heavy load of ammonia producing, oxygen consuming animals. We know that these words refer to the establishment of certain colonies of bacteria that convert toxic ammonia into less toxic nitrite and nitrate. A well seasoned aquarium has, in addition, a healthy population of heterotrophic bacteria, protozoans, worms, and minute crustaceans called copepods, all of which consume decomposing material and detritus, with a resulting production of ammonia. The importance of this second group of organisms is often overlooked in deference to the almighty "good bacteria," *Nitrosomonas* and *Nitrobacter.* I know that it is entirely possible to maintain an aquarium for years with little more than the conviction that there are "good bacteria" and "bad bacteria," but that is not why you are reading this column. Nevertheless, since the establishment of *Nitrosomonas* and *Nitrobacter* is the focus of our efforts during the conditioning period, I will discuss them first.

Nitrosomonas convert ammonia to nitrite, and consume

a lot of oxygen in order to accomplish the conversion. They function at peak efficiency in a trickle filter where the oxygen supply is not limited as it is when they are submerged under water. *Nitrosomonas* are rapid colonizers, and very quickly establish themselves in an aquarium or filter.

Nitrobacter are not so quick to become established. It is they that make us wait and try our patience. While they are, perhaps, less oxygen limited than *Nitrosomonas*, they are definitely more sensitive and fragile. When the test kit finally reads zero nitrite, and the nitrate reading has risen, we know that *Nitrobacter* has become established.

Every aquarist has a personal recipe for establishing these bacteria. In essence, only two ingredients are necessary. These are ammonia and a culture of bacteria. The source of quantity of ammonia, and the source and quantity of bacteria is what varies in these recipes, and these qualities can really make the difference between waiting two weeks to cycle and waiting twelve weeks. The recipes can be divided further into two categories: the organic method and the inorganic method.

The organic method refers to all techniques in which the ammonia used is from an organic source, and the ammonia itself is linked with, or in, the presence of organic (carbon containing) compounds. The old fashioned technique of using a few hardy fish to run a tank in, fits this category. Though it works eventually, this technique was undesirable because it frequently took a long time to complete the cycle or, if bacteria was added to speed up the process, the resulting population of bacteria was only capable of handling the given fish load.

A better technique which was popular in south Florida about ten years ago was to employ about two or three dozen live bait shrimp to get things going. This provided the amount of ammonia to really season the tank to a high capacity, and the cycle occurred faster. Still, according to the proponents of inorganic conditioning, the presence of organic compounds in the water inhibits the establishment of *Nitrosomonas* and *Nitrobacter* by

In fact the best way to establish a reef aquarium is with live rock. Since no external biological filter is needed, there is no point to conditioning separate filters. The rock serves as the biological filter, as does any sand or gravel on the bottom of the aquarium.

promoting the growth of heterotrophic bacteria which compete for space with them. I can tell you that this assertion, while technically correct, comes into serious question in practice. For instance, the technique of conditioning with fresh, decomposing live rock would seem to be a bad method as it would tend to create a massive growth of heterotrophic bacteria which compete with *Nitrosomonas* and *Nitrobacter*, in theory. In practice this is not the case as such aquaria tend to cycle very quickly, in two or three weeks on average, which is on par with run-in periods for inorganic conditioning. I believe the reason for this might be that the fouling rock tends to promote on-site production of heterotrophic bacteria, while the dry filter experiences a simultaneous growth of *Nitrosomonas* because of the availability of ammonia produced by the heterotrophs in the tank. Actually, the only disadvantage I can see in this technique is that it starts the tank out with a very high nutrient load. I prefer to establish the rock in a separate aquarium, as I described in a previous column.

The inorganic method of conditioning an aquarium has been described in this magazine by a number of authors, but, since each has his own recipe (of course), I will discuss the method developed and researched by Scott Siddall, which he explained in an excellent article also in this magazine (*Freshwater and Marine Aquarium* Vol 10 #3, p. 4).

Inorganic conditioning involves the use of a source of ammonia in excess, and without any associated organic molecules, combined with innoculation of *Nitrosomonas* and *Nitrobacter*. In Dr. Siddall's method, three fifths of one gram of ammonium chloride per gallon of water used is added as a single dose, followed by innoculation of bacteria. A significant advantage is seen in this method as the volume of the aquarium is inconsequential, since the conditioning can be carried out using only the filter recycling water through itself. This is why I said "per gallon used" above. To determine the grams of ammonium chloride you need, multiple 3/5 times the amount of water in gallons that it will be mixed with. Ammonium chloride comes in a powdered form called reagent grade, and is available through pharmacies, chemical companies, universities, and janitorial supply houses, but may require a phone call or ten to locate. A liquid solution of ammonium chloride is available in pet stores, from Fritz Co., but I do not know the concentration. Dr. Siddall's recipe calls for 45 parts per million ammonia. If this could be accurately measured to determined from the solution's concentration, it could be used just as well as the solid ammonium chloride. The only confounding issue is that the Fritz solution has an accompanying set of directions outlining yet another recipe. If you wish, follow their recipe, it will work. But do not attempt to mix methods!

Two other important qualifications of the Siddall recipe need to be noted. First is that the ammonia is added as one dose and no more. Second is that bacteria may be added several times after the ammonium chloride. My own modification of Dr. Siddall's method is to add bacteria daily. The reason for this is that the high initial dose of ammonia is toxic to the bacteria we want to establish. Repeated innoculation assures that some bacteria will survive and grow. Later additions of ammonium chloride could be perceived to be a way to "add fuel to the fire," but actually they may inhibit the process by killing off *Nitrobacter.* This has been my experience. Personally, I do not believe that it is possible for *Nitrosomonas* to starve and die-off when all the ammonia is converted to nitrite. Perhaps some die, but I believe they can go dormant.

One may ask, "Why not use the whole tank to complete the cycle, rather than just the filter?" The answer is that the water used will ultimately contain a very high concentration of nitrate, and will consequently be very acidic. This water should be discarded and replaced with new water of the same specific gravity and temperature. Some aquarists have reported to me a peculiar phenomenon where the ammonia is converted to nitrite in a week to ten days, which is normal, but the nitrite fails to be completely converted, after an initial peak and significant decline, with the resulting accumulation of nitrate. The whole process just freezes with the following readings: ammonia, 0; nitrite, approximately 5ppm; nitrate, high. The characteristic acidification which occurs has never been a problem for me but, perhaps, in smaller volumes of water the effect may inhibit the establishment of *Nitrobacter.* I do not know how the addition of a buffer would affect the recipe.

A couple of final notes on this subject ... As I stated earlier, heterotrophic bacteria and other microfauna, play a significant role in the well seasoned aquarium. I do believe that in the future aquarists will consider them more important than the nitrifying bacteria in reef-type aquaria, while fish-only aquaria will still require large colonies of *Nitrosomonas* and *Nitrobacter*. The microfauna are intimately linked with the algae in reef tanks, and when good protein skimming and/or algae filtration is employed, the need for nitrifyers is greatly reduced. This is, of course, dependent on fish population and the quantity of food (nitrogen) inputs. I wish to again note that at Sea Kleer Reefs we have established reef aquaria using seeded live rock, without the need for any conditioning period for the display tank. The rock, fish, and invertebrates could be added in one day, though it should be emphasized that the conditioning methods outlined in this article are a much safer route to follow, particularly for the novice. I have read no data on the use of inorganic conditioning in freshwater tanks and would appreciate hearing from hobbyists who have tried it.

Here again I was hinting that wet dry filters are not needed.

Finally, I want to note the occasional occurrence of no nitrate build-up during an inorganic conditioning. A number of aquarists have reported to me that no nitrate build-up occurred, or that there was an initial rise in nitrate and then it was all consumed suddenly. If we bear in mind that this occurred in filters alone, or attached to tanks with nothing but water in them, we can see that what has happened is a sort of denitrification in a very aerobic environment. It should be clear from these experiences that there are organisms which have not been described or extensively investigated that play a role in the nitrogen cycle in nature and in our aquaria.*

*Tim Hovanec from Marineland (Aquaria Inc.) has made some discoveries in this regard that will change our understanding of who the players really are in the bacterial soup of our aquaria.

So many small variables can have big effects on the end results in our tanks (i.e., the water, salt, equipment, light, food, rock, etc.). The aquarist has to be careful about mixing ideas and methods from several sources, but at the same time be opened minded enough to experiment a little. After a little experimentation and a lot of experience, one comes to the realization that the best method is one's own.

Ah yes, the questions!

Q. I look forward to your column in FAMA each month since you usually identify solutions to problems I've been experiencing. My problems are typical of those new to the hobby of reef keeping such as: excessive algae growth of the wrong variety, ammonia and nitrite levels, lighting, etc.

I started a 38 gallon marine aquarium this past Christmas (a present) and converted it to a reef tank a couple of months after the nitrogen process had run its course. Needless to say the equipment I'm using now is totally different than what was originally purchased. I built two trickle filters. The first utilized a 10 gallon aquarium with glass partitions and filter media box. Since the filter is located in the enclosed cabinet below the tank, access was very difficult due to the available space that remained. After receiving several cut fingers, I built an acrylic unit designed for easy access and serviceability.

Trickle Filter, 300 gallons per hour. (Described in text.)

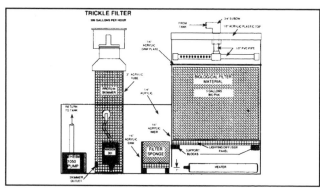

The tank contains 20 lbs. of live rock, a tube anemone, sea apple, two small shrimp, a 2 inch flame goby, a 2 inch damsel and eight *Turbo* Grazers. The trickle filter consists of 3 gallons of Bio-Pak, a rotating spray bar with a drip plate under it, and a foam filter block in the sump. Nothing is used in the wet section. The protein skimmer is powered by a 301 Hagen powerhead. An Eheim 1050 hobby pump is used. Make-up and 20% weekly water changes use reverse osmosis water. The foam prefilter is cleaned daily and the dolomite substrate is cleaned weekly.

Even with the maintenance schedule described above
and the light bio-load, slight ammonia and nitrite levels
are present when tested with my Dry Tab™ test kit. A
small amount of red algae would seem to support the
questionable water quality. Where have I gone wrong?
Am I moving too much water through the filter media?

Other questions that I need your help with are as follows: Do you recommend the use of activated carbon or
other chemical treatments in the trickle filter? How often
should I clean the filter block located in the sump of the
trickle filter? With 36 inch Actinic bulbs now available,
what arrangement do you recommend for my tank? You
discussed the use of inert substrate in past columns.
What do you use and where can I get it? Last, your feel-
ings on the use of ozone in a reef system. Sincerely,
Gary Nickerson, Wilbraham, Massachusetts

A. When I hear a question about a perpetual low level
of ammonia and nitrite, a few possibilities come to mind:

Double check your tests, the kits could be inaccurate. A
cured piece of coral purchased at the pet shop may not
have been completely cured and could have something
rotten in the core. Finally, a thick gravel or sand bed can,
in some instances, generate ammonia and nitrite. You
say that you have a dolomite substrate. How deep is it? I
do not believe that you can move too much water
through the filter, unless the dry portion becomes a wet
one because of the flow. I feel certain that the problem
is one of the three points I mentioned above.

I am including the drawing you provided because I'm
going to offer some constructive criticism on your filter
design that may make things a little easier for you. The
first thing that struck me in looking at your design was
that you were using both a spraybar and a drip plate.
There is no advantage to doing this — in fact the plate
defeats the purpose of the rotating bar. I would remove
one or the other, whichever is simplest for your design.
You have employed the weir and dam design that was
part of George Smit's original presentation. I do not like
this design because it partitions off the sump and greatly
reduces the amount of reserve water available to the

pump. In fact, for your filter to have a substantial reserve you would have to submerge part of the dry filter, which would significantly lower your filter's capacity. I am assuming that the filter sponge completely fills the space between the dam and weir, though the drawing shows a gap. If the gap exists, water would seek the path of least resistance and bypass the filter sponge. These problems could be solved by cutting through the acrylic dam, giving the pump access to the entire sump. Finally, the location of the heater makes it difficult to service. It would be better to place it on the other side of the sponge or by the pump. About your questions:

Notes: I no longer use a foam block or other mechanical filter media in the sump.

I do use and recommend activated carbon in the trickle filter. I use it mostly to remove the yellowing agents from the water. Yellow water is a filter that can effectively reduce the amount and spectrum of light reaching the specimens. You should clean the filter block in the sump about every three months when you change your carbon. You may either replace the sponge with a new one or rinse it out. If you do rinse it out, I suggest that you use saltwater only because these reticulated foam blocks typically develop a population of terebellid worms and simple syconoid sponges as well as flea-like amphipods. Freshwater would kill these and, while no disaster would occur, who really wants rotting spaghetti worms in his sump?

36 inch blue actinic bulbs are available from numerous companies now, and all give good results.

Philips has not made 36 inch Actinic bulbs yet. What you have seen is not a true Actinic bulb, but a copy. I have not tried any of the new copies yet. For now I recommend four 24 inch 40 watt high output Philips Actinic 03 and two 36 inch Sylvania daylight for your 36 inch tank. If you can fit more bulbs, do so. If you can make them all high output, do so. The daylight and Actinic bulbs should be alternated, and a four Actinic and two daylight combo would necessitate sandwiching the daylights, one between two Actinics.

On the subject of inert substrates, the foam block and Bio-Pak media are both inert, but if you are referring to gravel or sand, then I suggest silica.

By the way, time and again I have discussed the substrate in the bottom of our aquaria with respect to nutri-

I do not recommend silica sand. I prefer aragonite (calcium carbonate) sand or gravel commonly called coral sand. Sometimes commercially available coral sand mixes are cut with silica sand.

*Here my opinion was beginning to change as I began to realize that the benefits of the sand or gravel on the bottom could be realized without drawbacks if certain rules were followed.

November 1989

ent and detritus accumulation. It has been brought to my attention that many freshwater hobbyists and marine fish-only hobbyists have been concerned or upset by my recommendations for removing the gravel. This kind of confusion makes me angry because I try, in my articles and conversations, to make a point as clear as possible. C'mon folks, a little common sense, please? My recommendation for removing gravel is in reference to aquaria containing large amounts of live rock and filtered by a wet/dry system. In my experience removal of the bottom substrate optimizes results in this type of reef aquarium. I never intended to suggest that freshwater tanks and marine fish tanks should also be maintained without gravel. As a point of interest, I have been experimenting with some natural system (no filters or motors) aquaria and have found significant benefit to having a substrate in these.* I will report on these aquaria in future columns and in an article in preparation on the rearing of mandarin fish in captivity.

Ah yes, ozone. That is a subject I will discuss in detail next time, among other topics ... lighting again, perhaps.

'Till then ...

Let's just jump into the questions this month and skip all the introductory stuff.

Q. I am a rising ninth grade student at Porter-Gaud school in Charleston. For a science project next year, I plan to set up a 30 gallon reef tank containing many different types of coral. So I have a few questions: (1) I will have room for three bulbs (two daylights and one Actinic?). What wattages should I use? (2) Should I use food meant to be aimed directly at the coral to be fed, decreasing the amount of food received by corals that don't need to be fed? What types of corals do not need to be fed? (3) When I went snorkeling off the Florida Keys, I saw several beds of "Turtle grass" (is this a plant or a macroalgae?), but no macroalgae directly on the reef. Should macroalgae be used in a reef tank to decrease nutrients and, if so, should "macroalgae food" be added to the aquarium? Does macroalgae decrease the phosphate? Any other advice you have would be appreciated. Thanks, Braden McDaniel, Charleston, SC

A. I can think of a few better investments a school could make than a reef aquarium. I hope you will be receiving some support for your project because these systems can cost a bundle to put together, and as I've said before, it is generally best not to cut corners. Your project excites me a lot, and from the looks of the questions you ask it appears you have the maturity and aptitude to carry it off.

Times have changed. So have the options and so have my opinions. For this 36 inch tank I'd recommend the following options, either:
(1) 175 watt metal halide plus (2) 36 inch actinic, or
(1) 150 watt metal halide plus (2) 36 inch actinic, or
The above combinations using (2) metal halides instead of (1) or (3) 36 inch standard output full spectrum "daylight" fluorescents plus (3) 36 inch standard output blue fluorescents, or
(4) H.O. 36 inch fluorescents [(2) daylight spectrum and two blue] or (the bare minimum) (4) standard output 36 inch fluorescents [(2) daylight spectrum and two blue]

*This is true especially when the tank contains many fish that are

I am assuming that the reason you say you have room for only three bulbs is that you plan on using a few standard fluorescent fixtures. If this is your plan, consider changing plans for the following reasons: (1) You need more than three bulbs to have optimal results on a 30 gallon tank. (2) Some of these bulbs at least should be high output "HO," necessitating a ballast(s) not in the standard fixture, and (3) standard fixtures are awkward, heavy, and may retain heat in the hood. They also tend to rust. I am recommending that you use water resistant end caps instead. These will allow you to pack at least six bulbs across a twelve inch tank. With this arrangement I recommend four 2-foot 40w HO Philips Actinic 03, and two 3-foot Sylvania Daylights. The Daylights may be either standard 30w or HO, depending on your budget. Please note that I will have more to say on high output daylights later in this article. If you absolutely must use three bulbs only, I recommend two 2-foot 40w Actinic and one 3-foot Sylvania daylight.

Regarding the feeding of corals, every reef keeper has a special technique for doing or not doing this, and, of course, every way is the best way. I generally do not go out of my way to feed photosynthetic corals. I feed my fish such foods as live black worms, live brine shrimp, live grass shrimp, and frozen edible shrimp. Occasionally, a worm or a piece of shrimp will be dropped by a fish and snared by a coral. Believe me, this doesn't send me running for the nearest tweezers. Most photosynthetic hard corals will greedily accept food, but this does not mean that they should be fed. Aquarists who have been keeping photosynthetic coral for many years generally come to the conclusion that they need not be fed much at all.* Please recall that corals continu-

being fed. If the tank has few fish or if nitrate and ammonia are very limited by protein skimming, denitrification, and algal filtration, then feeding is very important for the corals.

Other notes: **feeding photosynthetic corals will promote their growth and encourage repair of injured tissue, providing this feeding does not pollute the water (i.e. when protein skimming and denitrification promote stable pH.)**

Dendronephthya **species feed on phytoplankton, which may explain the difficulty with keeping them in aquaria. It is also possible that other soft corals utilize this food source. (See Fabricius, K.E., Benyahu, Y., and A. Genin, 1995. Herbivory in Asymbiotic Soft Corals.** *Science.* **268, 7 Apr. Pp. 90-92)**

ously reel in their surface mucus with its abundant growth of nutritious bacteria as well as detritus. Some corals do need to be fed, however, and all of these corals are nonphotosynthetic, i.e., they have no zooxanthellae. This group includes the orange cup coral *Tubastrea* sp., the colorful *Dendronephthya* soft corals, and those gorgonians or sea fans which have white polyps or colored polyps, other than brown or green. One of the best foods for all of these is live brine shrimp nauplii, fed to the specimen by using a long tube or baster.

Turtle grass, *Thallasia testudinum,* is a true flowering plant, not an alga. You may grow it in an aquarium by collecting a section of "sod," preferably with some of the sediment, and transplanting the whole mass in the aquarium. Turtle grass needs substrate around the roots - - at least three inches for good results, and preferably fine sand. Turtle grass also needs fairly bright light. In this case, metal halide would be the best choice, though VHO (very high output) fluorescents would work as well. At certain times in the year the seeds of *Thallasia* may be found washing up on the beaches in Florida, often sprouting a couple of blades. These survive extremely well in an aquarium, and are easier to manage than a whole section of sod.

Algae in the reef tank or in a separate filter do decrease the nutrient levels, but if they are used for this purpose only, they should be harvested often. No, "macroalgae food" should not be added, in my opinion -- kind of like pouring more water on the floor while trying to mop up a water spill from a leak that can't be stopped. Yes, macroalgae decrease phosphate levels in the water, but if they are allowed to remain in the system and decompose, the phosphate is returned to the system.

Q. What are the comparative levels of phosphate in saltwater mixes? Lewis Lucas, Allentown, Pennsylvania

A. I've been getting this question a lot lately, and I have a surprising answer for you! I don't think it matters how much phosphate is in the salt, within reason, because the phosphate used is inorganic, and is rapidly assimilated by plants or blown off and out of the system by the protein skimmer. Inorganic phosphate stimulates rapid plant growth, but is not what causes the bloom of undesirable algae, in my opinion. I said "within reason" above because excessive inorganic phosphate additions (fertilization) could promote the accumulation of organic phosphate, and this would be detrimental. I agree that it would be best if the salts didn't have any phosphate at all, but I worry about the potential for abuse of this parameter in advertisements, with the possibility of inferior salts being touted as choice simply because no phosphate was added in manufacture.

Q. I have been keeping tropical fish for a couple of years now. I recently became interested in reef tank aquaria. My question is this: how do I start out right? I plan on using Actinic and Sylvania Daylight fluorescents in the intensity you recommend in your April '89 edition of Reef Notes. I have been reading everything I can get my hands on concerning reef tanks. I just finished Dr. Emmens' book *Miniature Reef Aquarium in Your Home.* Dr. Emmens does not go into detail about ozone in his book and I am confused on whether or not it is a necessity in a system like mine. I also have fairly hard water in my home and I may have some copper pipe in my house. Would reverse osmosis be beneficial?

My last question is: I understand biological filtration is greatly dependent on oxygen content. If I added an airstone under my biological filter containing Bio Balls, would I receive increased filtration?

I look forward to reading Reef Notes every month, and if you would answer my letter in FAMA it would put the finishing touch on all my hard work. Thank you. Ronald Eldridge, Houston, Texas

A. I promised last month I would talk about ozone this month and, so I will. First I want to recommend a book to you, Ron, and everyone else with a piece of the reef at home. Get yourself a copy of Martin Moe's latest, *The Marine Aquarium Reference, Systems and Invertebrates.* It is the kind of reference that has been needed for a long time, written in a style that captures Martin's personal charm, and covering all subject areas in a manner that doesn't scare people out of the water.

Ozone. There's another subject for controversy. I'll skip the introductory stuff of what ozone is and how it is made, and concentrate on its application in aquaria. It is no wonder that many hobbyists are confused about ozone because there are two schools apparent in the literature. One has it that ozone separates the men from the boys in reef keeping, the other has it that ozone is not necessary. In truth you need not use ozone to have a healthy reef tank, but you might have better results if you did use it. I see a real problem in the use of ozone and the associated meters and controllers in that it is possible for the aquarist to lose sight of the reason for using these devices, and become too involved in their operation. I have spoken to many hobbyists who complain about a redox reading, when their tank looks fantastic, or boast of the high redox value the meter displays, when their tank looks terrible. By no means do I wish to suggest that this equipment is useless. Rather, I am trying to drive home the point that we should not forget that our goal is to keep and grow a section of coral reef. With that in mind, one can apply ozone and observe the effect it has on the organisms, and if one has a redox meter one can take notes on how the tank looks at different levels, and choose a best level for that aquarium.

Ozone is applied either in a protein skimmer or in an oxygen reactor. In either case the effluent water should be filtered through activated carbon to remove residual ozone and some potentially toxic compounds generated by ozone treatment. The carbon should be replaced about once every one to three months. One should also be sure to filter the air blowing out of the skimmer with carbon, or to vent this air outdoors via a length of silicone hose. Ozone is said to enhance protein skimming, but I take a different view on what it does. Depending on the contact time of the protein skimmer, small doses of ozone do tend to make the skimmer generate more foam, but it is noticeably lighter in color when the foam collapses into a liquid, than when ozone is not being applied. Ozone oxidizes the compounds that stick to the bubbles in a protein skimmer, hence the "bleached" appearance of the liquid collected. While the volume of stuff collected in the cup might be increased by low doses of ozone, I do not think that this is indicative of more being removed from the system by the skimmer. I think the extra volume is water. In fact, higher doses of ozone can be shown to impede the collection of foam up to a point where no foam will form at all. This is because the ozone is oxidizing the compounds so completely that they no longer stick to the bubbles. It may sound like I'm dissuading the use of ozone, but actually I am not. When the compounds are oxidized by the ozone they are broken down into simpler molecules that may blow off out of the tank, be removed by the carbon, or be more quickly processed by the biological filter. In essence, some folks burn the stuff, while others show it off as brown gunk in a cup.

Ozone may be used periodically (a few days per month only) to remove the yellow color from the water. This techniques is particularly useful for giant public aquariums where the use of activated carbon for water decolorization is less practical.

How much ozone should be used? Well, if one is applying the ozone in a typically sized protein skimmer with plenty of activated carbon afterward, I don't think it is possible to overdo it with the ozone generators typically used (i.e., up to 100 mg/h). If one plans on using a very large protein skimmer (in excess of three feet) and high levels of ozone, plan on including a redox controller to be sure not to overdo it. The same holds true for oxygen reactors because of the high contact with ozone that they afford. Oxygen reactors are pressurized cylinders into which both ozone and water are injected, and the water's progress is slowed by media like Bio Balls to increase the gas/water contact. With a good oxygen reactor and redox controller, one can have very precise control of the redox potential of the water, which means that one can maintain the purity of the water despite the varied production and introduction of pollutants in the system. For some hobbyists there is no better method, and to look at some of their tanks, the opinion is justified. Still, you can put someone in the finest race car (John B's analogy), and this has no bearing on who wins the race. The art of aquarium keeping can be assisted by technology, but not replaced by it. If you must know, I do not use ozone in my systems mostly because I have noticed that ozonated systems tend to run elevated levels of nitrate, while systems using continuous, well maintained protein skimming or algae filtration tend to have much lower nitrate levels, and redox values in excess of 300mv. Even at nitrate levels of 15 to 20 ppm in ozonated systems the specimens do not appear to be adversely affected, so my reasoning may seem unfounded. As I've said before, to each his own.

Yes, reverse osmosis would be beneficial for filtering your tap water. You might also consider ion-exchange filters as a supplement or an alternative. Many hobbyists add an airstone under the dry chamber or simply pump air into the dry section, reasoning that it should facilitate the nitrification process by providing continuous oxygen availability at high concentration. Some hobbyists leave the air off during the day to conserve CO_2 for the plants, and turn it on at night to rid the system of excess CO_2. In this manner they can achieve a slight pH regulatory effect. I have heard hobbyists claim that adding air to the dry section raised the redox potential, and that when the air was removed, the redox plummeted. Perhaps this is true, but I am skeptical and I'll tell you why. As the water drains down the pipe to the dry filter it carries a lot of air with it, so much so that it creates a positive pressure in the dry section anyway. Maybe more rapid ventilation than this has a special effect. It is possible that rapid ventilation assists the "cracking" off of the fraction of ammonia which can escape to the atmosphere.

*This is no longer my opinion. I now use and recommend metal halide lights, which have improved a lot since then. Also, the recognition that trace elements are critical in the maintenance of coral pigmentation solved the mysterious problem of "burning" and bleaching which seemed to occur eventually with metal halide lights after initial good results. With trace element supplementation this is no longer a problem.

Well, it's time I started talking about the photographs, but first a little history. As we all know, there is a perpetual battle in the available literature and journals over which type of lighting is best for captive reef systems. I too have played a role in this battle because I have written a few articles stating my opinion based on my observations with particular light sources. It has been my contention that metal halide lamps are not the best choice for small captive reef systems*, especially if one's goal is to grow hard coral. I am writing about this again now because I have seen new evidence that hard corals can do well under metal halide light *under certain circumstances,* and because I now have photographic proof of the positive short-term, and negative long-term effects of metal halide light in one aquarium. I am also including a hypothesis to explain the results with metal halide, and some important information about fluorescents.

*I was being facetious here...I didn't really consider it astounding.

**I no longer consider Porites difficult...it simply needs very bright light.

***I was wrong! Infra red can cause burning in corals if they are 2 or 3 inches away from a metal halide bulb or if they fall under the "hot spot" a few inches under a pendant metal halide, but I.R. did not cause the problem I was describing. Another poison did, however. It was oxygen. Too much oxygen was building up in the coral's or anemone's tissues as a result of photosynthesis by their symbiotic zooxanthellae. This problem occurred with metal halide lights because they were so bright that they stimulated more rapid photosynthesis than fluorescent lamps. Trace elements seem to assist in the detoxification of the excess oxygen.

Although I was completely wrong about the cause, I am still glad

Let's start out with my astounding* admission that hard corals can do well under metal halide lamps given certain conditions. Several months ago I visited the National Zoo in Washington for the first time, and there I saw a very interesting reef exhibit in the invertebrate house. The zoo maintains a reef in a tall acrylic aquarium lit by two Sylvania metal halide lamps and filtered by -- are you ready folks? -- an undergravel filter with crushed coral and shell -- that's it! Yes, the bottom is covered with red slime algae (cyanobacteria) as one might expect, but while the tank left a lot to be desired as far as aesthetics go, the inconceivable was occurring right before my eyes. There on the bottom towards the back were a few pieces of *Porites astreoides* that were not only showing their lovely bushy polyps, but also were growing! Thin, flat veneers like terraces were coming off one piece. Also, the "open brain" coral, *Trachyphyllia,* at the bottom of the tank was doing well, as were the numerous soft corals. Some lovely corallimorpharians, *Ricordea florida*, at the bottom, near the *Porites,* were fully expanded. I was astounded, mostly by the *Porites* because it is very difficult to keep in the long run.** (It should be noted that the aquarist at the zoo perform frequent, large water changes on this aquarium.)

Imagine, if you would, group of starving animals being offered their favorite food, and how positively they would respond. Now imagine that the person feeding these animals has placed a little poison in the food, and that this poison has a slow, cumulative effect. I believe that this analogy closely parallels the use of metal halide light on certain organisms. I should also have added that some of the animals are immune to the poison while others suffer to varying degrees. The poison I allude to is infra red light and, perhaps, far red light, again in my opinion. These would be filtered out with sufficient depth of water to a point where their intensity is sufficiently reduced to render them harmless, or where they don't penetrate any further.***

The photos taken by Lourdes Vizcarrondo show the effects of this poison on a beautiful reef tank owned by Santiago Gutierrez. Photo #1 shows some uncommon corallimorpharians, *Rhodactis (Discosoma) sanctithomae,*

Top: Initially the *Rhodactis* responded positively to the light. *Bottom:* But then they shrivelled up...see above sidebar comments for explanation.

and the lovely encrusting soft coral, *Briareum asbestinum.* This photo was taken when the specimens were relatively new to the tank. Notice how well they are responding to the light.

Photo #2 is a "pan" to the right, showing some *Ricordea florida,* upper left, two *Eunicea* sp. gorgonians, center and bottom right, and some *Palythoa caribbea,* center. In time, however, the negative effects occur.

In Photo #3 we see that the *Rhodactis* is shrunken and the *Briareum* is shriveled. Also note the appearance of the *Palythoa,* upper right, like a boiled potato. Santiago had been very pleased with his tank for a while, but he began calling me and telling me that things were not doing so well as before. I made a suggestion. "Do me a favor, Santiago," I said. "Trust me and turn off your metal halide for just a few days, put on some Actinics, and call me to tell me what happens." Santiago called back quite impressed, and sent me the photographic record of some dramatic improvement. At first Santiago used only 50 watts of Actinic on his two foot cube tank, and he noticed a big improvement in only three days. Then he added two daylights and two high output Actinics, which is the lighting combination in Photos #4 and #6. Santiago is now further increasing his lighting with high output daylights and more high output Actinics.

Photo #3 was taken June 6, 1989 under metal halide. Note the improvement in Photos #4 and #6, taken on June 17. Observe the improvement in size and color of the *Rhodactis,* and note the appearance of the feathery gorgonian, *Pseudopterogorgia* sp. and the *Briareum.* Compare the polyp expansion in Photos #5 and #6. Interestingly, Santiago said that the hard corals in his tank (note: mostly at the bottom or shaded) did not seem harmed by the metal halide. It is difficult to guess if the damage would have occurred eventually or not. At any rate, the corals continue to do well now. Santiago tells me that the corals were all collected in less than ten feet of water. Photo #7 is a shot of the zoo aquarium taken by Charles Delbeek. Note the two large *Sarcophytons,* and the lovely *Sinularia* sp. (top rear). I'm sorry I don't have a photo of the growing *Porites* -- you'll have to take my word or see

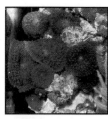

Above: The *Rhodactis* are looking better with less intense light. See text.

Some of the photos could not be reproduced. Please refer to the original column.

*I do not know for sure whether the effect I observed in my tank was due to UV only or again to buildup of toxic oxygen in the most heavily illuminated branches. The UV shield removed UV and lowered the light intensity.

for yourself -- Charles' camera malfunctioned, darn it!

My hypothesis about infra red has not been proven yet. Let's all see how long it takes someone to be selling infra red filters for metal halide lamps.

I wanted to tell you about some interesting effects I witnessed in my own tank recently. My aquarium had been lit by a combination of high output Actinics and standard output daylights, and was very successful with this combination, but a few months ago I decided to try high output daylight bulbs on my tank, and I found that my formerly bushy gorgonians showed "bald spots" on the portions exposed to the most light within three inches of the surface of the aquarium. I thought they were responding to the change in light intensity, as corals will, but they did not adapt. It was amazing. Branches bending near the surface had no polyps out on top, but were fully expanded on the shaded side. Then I looked at the spectral output of daylight bulbs, and noticed a significant ultraviolet peak. Shortly thereafter I slid a UV-absorbing lens over the bulbs and, presto, the polyps came out again in two days, after having been closed for over two months! Now they are always expanded.*

What does this teach us? First, since the standard daylights did no harm, the greater intensity of the UV radiation in the HO daylights was able to penetrate deeper into the water. This idea could be applied to metal halides and infra red as well. Metal halides vary in intensity, and this fact may be partly responsible for the battle waged in aquarium publications. Second, the high output Actinics did no harm, indicating that their UV output is negligible or non-existent, as I have been told by Philips, and have said before in this column. Considering the real ultraviolet output of bulbs commonly used in the home or office (i.e., Daylight, Vita Lite™), I think it is ludicrous to suggest that Actinics are harmful. Nevertheless it should be known that staring directly at any type of bulb should be avoided just as staring at the sun should be avoided. Intense light does harm the eyes. Have no fear, staring at your aquarium for hours each day does no harm at all, aside from preventing you from doing that assignment that's due tomorrow!

Q. I recently reread your column in the February 1989 issue of FAMA concerning the anisogamous sexual reproduction in *Caulerpa* macroalgae. By coincidence, the process was occurring in my tank at the time. I have made one observation which may shed a little light on the causes of this type of reproduction. My tank is a newly established 75 gallon "standard" marine aquarium, not a reef tank. It has an undergravel filter and Magnum 330 filter with a floss sleeve and charcoal canister. The tank was near the end of its initial cycling period, with a pH of 8.1, ammonia 0, nitrite 0.25 mg/L, nitrate 20 ppm, temperature 80° F, and specific gravity of 1.024. The light is provided by two 4' fluorescent fixtures with standard (no Actinic) tubes. The only life in the tank at the time of the reproduction were three *Chrysiptera taupou*.

I was given several small rocks with "starters" of *Caulerpa racemosa*. I placed them in the tank and added some Coralife® Aquatic Plant Food according to the directions. Most of the plants are flourishing after four days; one died shortly after being put in the tank, turning limp, dark, and shriveling up. I removed the dead one.

The plants had been in a plastic bag in the dark for about two hours before being placed in my aquarium. In removing the plants, I found several loose pieces which had broken off. Most of these I discarded, but one, which was about 2" long and looked healthy, I decided to try to save. It had a small piece of horizontal "runner" about 3/4" long. I planted this in the crushed coral bottom of the tank, burying the runner just deep enough to keep the plant from floating away. I am aware that this is not the correct way of placing this plant, but I was curious as to what might happen.

Within 24 hours, this plant showed the signs of anisogamous sexual reproduction as you described them: the plant turned pale and blotchy, with a network of green covering it. About 48 hours later, I observed the discharge of the green material and watched the now ghostlike white plant turn limp. Fascinating! My question is this: Is it possible that the damage to the horizontal runner, and my subsequent placing it in the crushed coral substrate, might have triggered the reproductive cycle? Perhaps there is some special need of the horizontal runners for circulating water or light. The temperature, light level, chemistry, and salinity of the water do not appear to be factors in this case, since the other plants in the tank are healthy and are growing rapidly.

Many thanks for your interesting column in an excellent magazine. Sincerely, The Rev. John E. Borrego, Lawton, Oklahoma

A. I've decided that what really causes my *Caulerpa* to go into reproduction is that I stare at it too much. It's a sure thing that if you keep on looking at it, the plant will eventually go limp. I'm just kidding, of course, but to tell you the truth, there's not much more I can add to what I said before in my column. I would like to emphasize the fact that *Caulerpa* must be pruned often, and that such pruning definitely prevents reproduction. In my tank I regularly prune back *Caulerpa* so much that very little remains. I allow it to become conspicuous when I expect to be showing the tank off, but I never allow it to grow very dense. As far as how I go about trimming the plants, I usually use small scissors once per week. The plants seem to "leak" less when trimmed this way, though I have never witnessed any harm done by "*Caulerpa* juice." I promptly remove and throw away each section of plant that I have cut off. I trim my *Halimeda* this way too, though it only needs pruning about every two weeks.

There are a couple of things I want to comment on regarding your observations. You noticed initially that one of the plants turned limp and dark shortly after being placed in the tank. This condition occurs when *Caulerpa* loses "pressure." It may be caused by a dramatic change in specific gravity which exceeds the plant's ability to osmoregulate — either the cell wall bursts and the plant goes limp, the plant from less dense water loses water to the tank, or it may occur when there is significant damage to the cell wall. *Caulerpa racemosa* is particularly sensitive to kinking of the rhizoid in handling, and thus damaged portions often die as you described. I have wondered, too, about the potential effect of important osmoregulatory ions such as calcium on plants during acclimation. Great differences in water hardness might also play a role in the loss of pressure.

I do not think that water circulation and light effects on the runner (or the lack of these) produced the reproduction you observed, but your suggestion shows some creative thinking, and I like that. Hey, you might be correct about this, but I'll tell you why I don't think so. I have observed numerous species of *Caulerpa* growing where only the upright blades were visible, and the rhizoids were in black, anaerobic sand. These include *C. prolifera, C. mexicana, C. cupressoides,* and *C. sertularioides.* In fact, one species, *C. languinosa,* virtually always grows with the rhizoid buried in the sand. I have never found *C. racemosa* with its rhizoid buried in the sand, so you may have a point.

So, you might ask, why do I think the one piece went into reproduction while the others were unaffected? Well, I think the answer may lie in the fact you noted that this piece was not attached to a rock, while the others were. It is not the detachment from the rock that I am pointing out, rather it is the separation from the "symbiotic" bacteria, protozoans, and other microorganisms that occur on the rock which may have played a role. The gravel would not have had a population of these yet.

Q. I have excellent success with soft corals in my tank, but the hard corals such as *Euphyllia* sp. and *Catalaphyllia* sp. slowly recede from their "shell." Other hobbyists with the same system as mine don't have the same problem. What makes coral tissue recede?

A. This question briefly compiles the numerous phone calls and letters I have received on this subject. I talked about this when I discussed the effects of organic phosphate on coral. To refresh the memory, I explained that phosphate is considered to be a "poison" in the calcification process, that is, it prevents the formation of calcium carbonate crystals. Now, phosphate is not the only cause for the tissue receding, but the following explanation which I am proposing (yes, another of my hypotheses) should make it clear why it can be a factor.

A little background information is needed before the hypothesis. Corals lay down calcium in layers. Each layer is begun with the secretion of an organic matrix by the coral. To give you a mental image, think of this matrix as looking like fiberglass screening, and know that it is composed of a mesh of filaments much like our own hair. The matrix provides the architecture or form onto which the crystals of calcium carbonate bind, ultimately determining the form of the particular species. The exact nature of this whole process has not been worked out completely, and I encourage anyone doing research on this at a university to send additional information, as it would surely benefit those who keep corals in captivity.

Now to my hypothesis. I believe that corals recede from their skeleton when some kind of disturbance causes them to lay down layer upon layer of this matrix on top of the old calcium carbonate until the tissue completely separates from the base. The most rapidly growing sections should begin to separate first, according to this hypothesis, and this actually is what is observed. It should be clear that if the coral is laying down the organic matrix, but something is preventing the formation of calcium carbonate crystals, whatever the cause, then the tissue will recede.

Some further qualifications are necessary to explain all examples of tissue recession. Physical abrasion or damage can make coral tissue pull away from a localized area, and subsequent growth of algae, sponge, or soft coral can prevent regrowth of tissue in the area. Physical and chemical attack by other corals can also cause tissue recession. This problem is a most disturbing one for those who keep coral in a closed system because the simple advice to give corals plenty of room will not prevent all types of "attack." Many soft corals release potent terpenoid compounds into the water which are inhibitory to coral growth. Finally, bristle or "fire" worms may hide during the day and feast on coral tissue at night — beware!

Of course there are diseases which attack corals, and these often cause a retreat of the tissue from the skeleton. Most notable of these is a very pesky protozoan which attacks both hard and soft corals, as well as zoanthid anemones and corallimorpharians. An infection with this protozoan leaves exposed white skeleton behind a progressing front of brown, jelly-like "tissue" in hard corals. Corals without a skeleton that have this infection either partially or completely dissolve under a coat of "brown jelly." Zoanthid anemones with a mild infection often exhibit degeneration of the tentacles. Many hobbyists believe that this protozoan only attacks corals that have already been damaged, but I disagree. I take a more cynical view, preferring to believe that it attacks merely to keep even the experts humble!

Two other notable diseases are "black band" and "white band" disease. Black band disease is caused by a blue-green alga, *Phormidium,* that appears to digest the tissue, leaving bare white skeleton behind a front of the dark alga. The exact cause of white band disease is not clearly defined, but it appears to be of a bacterial nature, and causes rapid disintegration of the coral tissue.*

A number of coral species exhibit a syndrome wherein the tissue rapidly recedes from the skeleton, but the polyps are left intact and continue to respond in a healthy manner. This condition fascinates me, and I sincerely hope to discover the mechanism and explanation for its occurrence. I suspect that the mechanism involves the secretion of the organic matrix. Perhaps the polyps are firmly anchored in their calyces via canals, preventing them from peeling up as well.**

To prevent tissue recession in those hard corals most often kept in hobbyist's reef aquaria, such as *Euphyllia, Catalaphyllia, Plerogyra,* and *Trachyphyllia* ("grape" and "hammer," "elegans," "bubble," and "open brain," respectively), I offer a few suggestions. Light intensity is critical to achieve proper calcification. Even when one uses the proper type of bulbs, if there is not enough intensity, the coral will eventually stop growing and will recede from its base. I think that inadequate lighting is the most frequent cause for tissue recession. Limiting sources and build-up of organic phosphate by the methods already outlined in previous columns will also prevent the occurrence of tissue recession. One more water quality parameter that may play a role in coral tissue

*Low alkalinity and low pH prevent calcification and are a significant cause of tissue recession. Alkalinity, measured as milliequivalents per litre meq/L should be about 2.5 to 3 meq/L, which corresponds to about 7 or 8 dKH.

recession is carbonate hardness. My advice on this parameter contradicts advice I have seen published elsewhere, so the aquarist will have to experiment for himself to determine what works best in his or her reef tank. I find that hard corals fare best at a carbonate hardness of around seven or eight degrees (German dKH). I have witnessed hobbyists whose aquaria have relatively high KH (in excess of 15 dKH), trying to rationalize that the reason their corals were popping out of "their shell" was because the carbonate hardness was not high enough. All I can offer is my assurance that every time I have measured carbonate hardness of natural sea water on sight at the reef, it has been between seven and nine, though usually closer to seven dKH.*

Prevention of coral disease, as I indicated above, is not an exact science, but a few suggestions might help. I have said before that temperature is critical for a successful reef aquarium. In my experience, reef building corals in captivity are stressed by temperatures above 80° F, and below 68° F. Avoiding these extremes, as well as temperature fluctuations, is necessary for optimal results. Water motion is also critical, allowing proper exchange of gases, nutrients, and waste metabolites. Improper water motion could weaken tissue to infection. Finally, one has to be aware that placing a hard coral downstream from a soft coral might be harmful to the hard coral, though complete prevention of this kind of stress is difficult in a closed system aquarium.

I have more to offer you regarding the "pesky protozoan" mentioned earlier, thanks to Charles Delbeek who discovered some information on it in a Dutch journal. The name of the beast is *Helicostoma (porpostoma) nonatum*. Strong water motion and siphoning off of affected tissue are recommended and, interestingly, it is also recommended that the aquarium be treated with a culture of another, predatory species of protozoan such as *Euplotes*. Charles told me that additional information may be obtained by writing to: H.R. Beul, c/o Het Zee - Aquarium, Postbus 45, 7680 AA Vroomshoop, The Netherlands.

In previous columns I have mentioned that I have been experimenting with natural system aquaria and, since I have some nice photos* to show you, I thought I'd tell you a bit about them. First is my 15 gallon reef tank. About 10 months ago I decided to take the dive off the cliff and I removed all of the media from my trickle filter. This left the tank filtered by a mechanical prefilter (a 4" x 4" polyester pad washed daily), a protein skimmer, and one unit of Chemi-Pure™ in the sump of the "filter." No disaster occurred, not even with heavy feeding, nor the loss of some cold water anemones I was holding. As I suspected, biological filtration in this reef tank was occurring within the rocks. If anything, the tank looked better to me. Now, I do not wish to imply that a reef tank should be set up without a filter. I merely wish to show that it can be done, and to add my two cents in saying that such a system can be quite stable — it is not teetering on the brink of failure. A fish-only tank without significant rock density would naturally be much more dependent on excess supplementary filtration. Just to add a little more risk to my system. I decided to try letting the water drain directly into the sump — no trickling except in the overflow. Three months later the tank remains solid and gorgeous, as can be seen in the photos. Granted, I do consider the protein skimmer an important element in this success, though I have other natural systems succeeding as well without a skimmer. A point in case is my "Chesapeake/Marsh/Mangrove swamp" tank which I set up with water from Solomons Island, MD, gravel from the wave beaten shore at Point Lookout, and plants from Florida, North Carolina, and various salty and semi-salty locations in Maryland. Animals include *Littorina* sp. snails from all of the above areas; mussels, tunicates, and amphipods from the Chesapeake; "ghost shrimp" from a local pet store; a school of Celebes Rainbowfish, a pair of Bumble Bee Gobies, and a Twenty Four Karat Platy. The tunicates were not collected, but appeared suddenly when the set-up was about a month old. I "established" the system with the ghost shrimp and snails in the first month. I suspect that the gravel, taken fresh from the water, had some beneficial organisms on it. Other exciting events in this tank include the complete reproduction of ghost shrimp, and the growth of *Dasya* sp. and *Ceramium* sp. algae from the gravel. A very key factor in the success of this aquarium is its placement in a window where it receives several hours per day of natural sunlight. The room it is in is air conditioned. There is no filter on this tank, only an open ended air supply to generate turbulence.

Finally, just above this tank in the window I have a 5' long wave tank which I set up with seeded live rock. It houses one happy Percula Clownfish, some corals, and some magnificent growth of algae, due to the surge and natural sunlight. An Eheim pump supplies water to the wave trough. There is no mechanical nor chemical filtration on the tank which contains barely two gallons of water. Algae species include *Laurencia* sp. (3 species), *Dictyota* sp. (3 species), *Dictyopteris* sp., *Sargassum* sp., *Acanthophora spicifera, Cymopolia barbata, Chamaedoris peniculum, Penicillus* sp., *Ceramium* sp., *Cladophora* sp., *Cladophoropsis* sp., *Avrainvillea* sp., and *Udotea* sp. (2 species), and my personal favorite, *Coelothrix* sp., which fluoresces blue in the sunlight. Many thanks to Dr. James Norris at the Smithsonian for some of the algae and thanks to Dr. Adey for the inspiration for the tank design.

I plan on connecting this tank with the 15 gallon tank across the room, if I can find the time.

Well, that about does it for this month. I'll be answering more of your questions next time.

February 1990

It's starting to get cold again, so many of you will be spending more time indoors slaving over your reef aquariums and savoring their tropical warmth and color, as the outdoor environment quickly fades into a cold gray and brown mush. Your local pet dealer will be glad to see you again, stranger, and I would be thrilled to get some pictures of your captive reef so that we might possibly share them with our readers.

In viewing a number of hobbyist's home aquariums, I was inspired to make some drawings on the computer in the hopes of showing how to stack the rocks properly. Bear in mind we are dealing with two dimensions for the sake of simplicity. When the specimens are in place, the distinction between the loose and brick construction is difficult to show on paper.

1. & 2. Front view of proper "loose" construction (1.) and "brickwork" (2.). Done properly, the loose structure can have ledges and caves.

1.

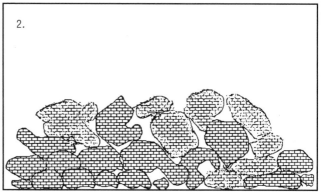

2.

3. A dramatic effect can be achieved when the reef is built in the middle of the aquarium. This offers viewing from both sides and around the end.

4. Proper construction as in (1.), viewed from the side.

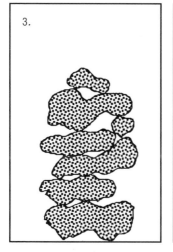

3.

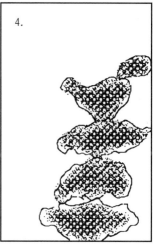

4.

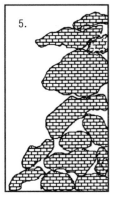

5.

Do not stack the rocks like bricks! Most of the reef tanks I have seen in people's homes have been built like this. While it is easier to construct such a wall, removal of accumulated detritus is impossible.

One need not just build a "wall", whether loose or not. Be creative! One can even attach small rocks or corals to the glass with underwater epoxy cement. For additional information about this and other aquascaping techniques please read *The Reef Aquarium, Vol1* by Delbeek and Sprung.

One should avoid creating a tight brick wall because such a structure impedes water circulation and traps detritus. The looser structure is much more difficult to assemble permanently, but affords better water quality in the long run. One may notice that the difference between these methods includes not only the style of assembly, but also the shape of the rocks used. Large flat rocks and oddly shaped rocks make it easier to avoid building a cobble wall. I always try to have a large open area behind the reef to allow fish to swim the full length of the tank under cover, and to allow easy siphoning of detritus. So many hobbyists begin the construction of their reef by placing rocks right up against the back glass of the aquarium, making access behind the reef impossible. Also, I try to minimize the number and size of points of contact with the bottom of the aquarium. What I am suggesting is that planning the reef structure is as important a consideration for the ultimate success and ease of maintenance of the aquarium as is the choice of filters, lights, and other equipment. As I have indicated before, the seemingly small variables really can add up to make a difference in our aquaria, not in an exact quantitative manner, but more in the sense of a qualitative art. Certainly the biology of the organisms provides an explanation for the success of applied art, but it is often difficult to thoroughly explain all the details that one considers after years of studying reef organisms.

Did I hear a question?

Q. Although I have been reading FAMA for a couple of years now, I have not seen a discussion on the subject of red algae with more than a passing reference to it and water quality. I would like a few more details; like how to get rid of it!

I just finished tearing down my 180 gallon tank because it became completely overrun with the stuff. I could clean it completely and the gunk would be back totally covering everything within two weeks. By this time I only had one blue damsel living in the tank and it had been the only inhabitant for the past four months. I was running a reverse flow system with a corner drain filled with Bio-Balls, through a Lifegard 12" filter series. This was all driven by a 3MD pump. Lighting consisted of four 30 watt Ultralume™ 50's. Also in place was a PVT-450 protein skimmer connected with an ozonizer. I also used Nitrex boxes(2), Chemi-pure™(2), and Poly Filter™.

Everything that I measured was normal: Ammonia 0, nitrites 0, pH 8.2, and nitrates 0. Nitrates have been the only odd thing, even when I had the tank full of fish. Different articles keep mentioning holding nitrates below 20-30 ppm, but I've never had any nitrates, zero. As you might suspect, trying to get rid of the red algae resulted in 30% water changes every 3 to 4 weeks for quite some time. I tried lots of ozone, no ozone, lights on all day, and lights off — all to no avail!

My damsel has been in my quarantine tank (10 gal.) for almost nine weeks and it's starting to get some red algae. It has had lots of green hair algae for most of its life with periods of up to four months without any fish. It sets in the kitchen and gets plenty of natural sunlight. Again, the readings are normal except pH stays about 8.2-8.4.

I want to set my 180 gallon back up with a normal filter system pumping 900+ gph using Bio-Beads™ or Matrix™ in an Ocean Clear™ filter system and not run an under-gravel filter at all; just cover the bottom with a thin layer of sand. I will put the Lifegard system on a 30 gal. tank I have and make an invert tank. How do I keep the red algae out of all of these? What should I be measuring that I'm not at the present that would indicate an onset of red algae, and what do you think about the nitrates? I realize this is too long to publish in its entirety, but thanks for any information or suggestions, and keep up the good work. Sincerely, Dan Kinman, Plano, Texas

P.S. In case you were wondering what happened to all of my other fish, we had a severe cold snap and I couldn't keep the tank temperature from dropping about 10 degrees last winter. Everyone got Ich or something similar and died except for the damsel.

A. Dan, I think I have given more than passing attention to this problem, as have other authors, but I do have some additional information for you that might help you find out how to "get rid of it." Before I get into that, however, I want to comment on your seemingly unusual disappearing nitrate. It is my understanding from Aquarium Products that a key ingredient in Nitrex media affects the accuracy of Nitrate test kits. Nevertheless, it can be demonstrated by other means that Nitrex media does work extremely well, as claimed.

The red beast that I have discussed in this column may represent a number of cyanobacteria (blue-green algae) species, but the most common one is probably *Schizothrix* sp.

I refer you to previous columns where I discussed this algae's affinity for calcium containing substrates, its use of organic phosphates, and its control via nutrient limitation and use of herbivores.

It intrigues me that you noticed the correlation between the addition of the damsel to the spare tank and the appearance of red algae. I have wondered if certain fishes' metabolic wastes stimulated such algae more so than others. I do know that certain invertebrates, particularly Octocorallia, tend to grow cyanobacteria on them because they leach organic compounds. Plants such as *Caulerpa* sp. may also tend to get covered by the red beast because of useful organic leachates.

Regarding your observations on ozone, I feel certain that you did not use it properly, or not enough for the size aquarium, because its use definitely does have an impact on the occurrence of cyanobacteria. I talked about ozone use in the November issue. Please re-read what I said then. I would like to hear from you again to get some quantitative data on how much ozone you used — "lots" or "a little" doesn't tell me very much. Some hobbyists feel that protein skimming causes red algae blooms, by the way. Their argument is that protein skimming supersaturates the water with nitrogen, and the cyanobacteria, because of their nitrogen fixing ability, are thus stimulated. While this seems a very reasonable hypothesis, I personally don't agree with it.*

*In my experience increasing protein skimming is one of the best cures for red slime algae.

While we're on the subject again —

Q. Recently over this last month. I have had a problem with a dark reddish brown slime-like algae. It covers all of the rocks, dolomite, macroalgae, and some of the invertebrates. I have noticed that as this brown algae slime covers a surface area, bubbles form underneath. How can I eliminate or control the brown algae slime? It is detracting from the appearance of the tank.

The second problem that I have noticed is my nitrate level likes to stay between 60 and 80 ppm. The twelve gallon water changes (on a 55 gal. tank) only bring it down to 20 to 30 ppm. My ammonia and nitrite levels are maintained at 0.0 ppm. The pH level is 8.2. The specific gravity is maintained at 1.021. The water temperature is maintained at 75 to 78 degrees. How can I control the nitrates? Will the nitrate destroy my invertebrates?

I have an Orbicularis batfish which grew from a fragile 1.25" to 10." His eating habits have changed. Will the batfish become a problem to the zoanthids and the mushroom coral?

I am using a dry/wet filter system modeled after the George Smit mini-reef filter. In the filter I am using DLS, calcite, activated carbon, and a protein skimmer. I am also using a Magnum 330 as a carbon filter and for additional water flow. Cordially, Eric Blackman, Ellicott City, MD

A. I promise the folks out there concerned that I will not run the red algae issue in the ground. A lot of hobbyists still ask me this question, and unfortunately, I cannot print all of these letters. I printed these because they contained other items of interest.

For instance, here again a hobbyist is concerned with nitrate. Eric, I am confused about the twelve gallon water changes being able to dilute the nitrate to less than half its usual strength. Still, you might be performing them often enough to do just that. I suspect that part of the problem may be high nitrate levels in the tap or well water you might be using. What this would do is to give your tank an initially high nitrate level which would climb not only as you fed the tank, but also as you added water to make up for evaporation. With the typically high evaporation rates of these miniature reef aquariums, it is easy to see that nitrate could accumulate rapidly unless the make-up water is nitrate free. A good deionization unit for the tap, perhaps along with, or instead of, a reverse osmosis unit, would solve that problem. The elevated nitrate levels won't do your inverts any good, but the zoanthids and mushroom coral (I am assuming corallimorpharians) are tolerant of extremes that would slowly kill more sensitive organisms such as hard coral.*

*I have found that nitrate itself is not harmful to corals. The depleted alkalinity and low pH often associated with the formation of nitrate from ammonia is what is harmful.

Regarding the batfish, a hungry 10" specimen could certainly push the nitrate levels up in a 55 gallon tank! I don't expect the fish to bother your invertebrates, though one never knows. I have witnessed juveniles of the closely related Atlantic spade fish nibbling on coral mucus, not harming the coral, but definitely irritating it enough to make it close down.

A couple of changes in your system would make some noticeable improvements, and might solve the slime algae problem. Avid readers of this column already know that I'll advise: (1) Remove the dolomite substrate from the tank. (2) Remove the calcite from the wet section of the filter, and replace it with the carbon you have been using in the Magnum. This would leave the Magnum empty — that's fine, and it would make it easier to change the carbon every three months as you should. I promise you that these changes would not disrupt the biological filtration of the aquarium. They can be performed rapidly, and the improvements would be obvious within a few days. Good luck!

Q. In response to your February article in FAMA: The subject of reproduction in macroalgae is a reasonably complex one. The only answer I can give is that when there is an excess of CO_2 combined with a rise and fall of O_2 concentration, the reflex reproduction is observed by myself. In systems with low CO_2 plus constant O_2, reproduction does not appear to be prevalent!

In response to your April article in FAMA: I keep many kinds of corals in my reef tanks. Of these, *Goniopora* are one of my favorites. My experience with them is excellent! Did you know that most types of *Goniopora* can be

found in turbid water off fringing reefs as well as clear
water of outer reefs? I do not feed any invert food in my
tanks at all. They do survive and thrive in the wild under
very trying conditions. My specimens were obtained in a
poor condition and took some three months to grow
back new polyps where the collector's hand had
removed and damaged parts of the coral.

Conditions in my tanks are as follows: PO_4 0.02 ppm,
NO_3 0.05 ppm, SO_2 0.00 ppm, O_2 6-7.5 ppm, (low-
high), Fe 0.05 ppm, CO_2? — auto CO_2 not used yet, KH
15 degrees German, pH 7.9-8.4 (low to high), S.G. 1.022.

System:
Aquareef 70 gal. model with Bio-Balls, no gravel in the
sump, Dupla carbon in the sump. No ozone used. No
skimmer used. No O_2 reactor used. Lighting is 3 x 65w
Sylvania Super Blue Diazo Actinic, 3 x 36w Osram
lumilux 11 Daylight 6500K (3300 lumens each). Water is
R.O. Deionized and 1/2 micron post filtered and pol-
ished with carbon. Water change is 20 liters/week. No
gravel in the tank. Temperature is 76 to 80 (winter to
summer). No chiller is used.

Notes/Observations:
Tentacular extension on *Goniporas* reaches 7-8 inches.
Most common algae are *Halimeda* and crustose
corallines. Some *Valonia* bubbles (large 1" +). Soft corals
grow on bottom glass, side glass, and front glass.
Goniopora is very aggressive to most corals except perhaps *Physogyra, Plerogyra, Stoichactis*. I feel it is not
sensitive to other corals' slimes. I feel it does not need
invert food. The *Goniopora's* are nearly two years in
captivity and now totally healed from diver inflicted
injuries and grown onto the rocks adjacent to them! In
my opinion, *Goniopora's* need superb, 300+ mv water
quality, low in organics, reasonable temperature, high
O_2, medium CO_2 Actinic + Daylights (5,000-10,000 lux),
and also the most important aid, "a dedicated coral
enthusiast!"

In closing, Julian, I believe you are the finest writer in
the USA today, and most definitely the best ever FAMA

contributor! Congratulations, mate! Regards, Owen R. Jeffries Minireef Consultant Proprietor, Coral Reef Systems South Australia

A. I believe your success, Owen, but I want to show everyone, so send me pictures that we can share with our readers.

I would like to see more quantitative data on your assertions about *Caulerpa* and *Goniopora*. Again, I believe you, recalling the comments about qualitative art I made earlier in this month's column, but if you are going to make an assertion, some quantitative data gleaned from experimentation would make me feel more confident in your hypotheses.

I am jealous because where you live you can easily obtain a closely related coral *Alveopora*. The common name is "she love me not daisy" coral, and it is more spectacular than *Goniopora* species, in my opinion. It has not been offered for sale in the USA as of this writing. With the success you've been having, I'm sure you could keep it.

I'm really excited about your having *Goniopora* grow on to the rocks adjacent to it! As you noted, your dedication to your aquarium is a most important factor in this success. Thanks for the letter and compliments. I guess I print hobbyists' compliments to show what a self-centered, truly immodest guy I really am! Gosh!

Before I go, I'd like to give credit where credit is due. It is my understanding from Eddy Steinman of the Florida Marine Aquarium Society that he started the crazy technique of using live bait shrimp to cycle an aquarium. As I indicated in a previous column, the technique works quite well, and is really inexpensive if you live in Florida, or along the coast where you can easily get the little buggers.

'Till next time, keep tropical

I'm writing you folks from Toronto Canada, where it's bloody cold outside even now as we speak. The Marine Aquarium Society of Toronto invited me up here to do a tour of the tanks, and I've really enjoyed their enthusiasm and hospitality. I always like seeing hobbyists' reef tanks because each one has some very distinctive, sometimes personal qualities. Also, it is fascinating to see what dramatic differences are made by such subtle qualities as the type of rock, the way it is stacked, the routine of maintenance, water used, foods used, supplements, lighting, etc., Then, of course, there are always the rare and unusual specimens which can make a reef really unique. In the upcoming year I hope I can feature some of your reefs in my column.

I've been getting some feedback regarding the photographs of Santiago Gutierrez's reef tank, so I will clarify a few points that I neglected to cover in that column. Since I assumed that everyone realized that Metal Halide light sources emit substantial amounts of U.V. light, and that such fixtures typically are equipped with U.V. absorbing lenses, I discussed the infra red concern only. What has been pointed out to me though, is that not everyone realized this and, in fact, there are Metal Halide fixtures being sold with ultraviolet admitting lenses, or with no lenses at all. I wish to re-emphasize the fact that Metal Halide does not refer to one particular lamp, so the results achieved vary as greatly as there are types of bulbs and fixtures.

Additional feedback about this column suggests to me that many hobbyists read it under the assumption that I was writing an anti-Halide, pro-Actinic article. Those who read carefully understood that my purpose was to show in photographs the potential harm that can occur with Metal Halide, since no one had ever done so before, as well as to point out that there are definitely incidences of success with Metal Halide lighting, not only with soft corals and plants, as has been well documented, but also with hard corals.*

*My comments here sound odd now, but back then there was a commonly held belief in North America that metal halide was best for soft corals and fluorescents were best for stony corals.

As a final note on the subject of that column, Santiago is experimenting again with his aquarium's lighting. He will be using the Metal Halide lamp once again to observe if the same trend occurs, and will subsequently be adding a filter which blocks both infra red and U.V., followed by the final test with a filter that blocks U.V. light only. I look forward to presenting his results and accompanying photographic record some time this year.

Q. Please comment on the types of ballasts you have had luck with powering the Actinic bulbs. I tried a standard 40 watt ballast "Benchlite" to power two Actinic 03 24" 40 watt bulbs. The ballast got hot! After a short period it would shut down. A small cooling fan would keep it running, but after about a month it burned out producing a foul smell — the ballast that is.

Obviously, with the increasing numbers of H.O. bulbs of various lengths and wattages, a table detailing acceptable ballasts and suppliers would be useful. Many people I have spoken with about this seem to have had a similar problem. Perhaps you could help. Thank you, Mark Widick, Nashville, Tennessee

A. Obviously, such a table would be useful, that is why I included one in my column in the April 1989 issue of this magazine. I'm beginning to learn that it doesn't pay to give people an answer before they ask the question. What you ask concerns me because, as you point out, you are not alone. I noticed a long time ago that there was a tendency for hobbyists to hook up high output and very high output bulbs with the wrong ballast. What really concerns me is the hobbyists' innocence at installing a potential fire hazard in the home. Often the problem lies in the ignorance of someone at a hardware store. Frequently we have a more serious problem, and that is someone at the pet store not knowing the proper ballast for a given bulb. I do not wish to offend those helpful folks at your pet store, who are well informed, especially since they are probably the ones reading this. The other guys in the industry make it tough for hobbyists like you, Mark, to do the job right. So, it's up to you to keep well informed. Get some books if you haven't already done so, be skeptical, and have an open mind.

I can tell you that 24" high output bulbs require an 800 milliamp high output ballast. Do not be fooled by the wattage! This ballast will say, "60 watt, High Output," and give you a minimum bulb length. I recommend the ballast made by Universal Magneteck. The ballast will get pretty hot, but it will not fry like the one you experienced. Remember folks, high output bulbs with the letters H.O. need high output, 800 mA ballasts. Very high output bulbs with the letters V.H.O. need very high output, 1500 mA ballasts. Bulbs do light up even when connected to the wrong ballast, so this is not a criteria of proper usage.*

*Now there are also electronic ballasts available for H.O. and V..H.O. bulbs, and manufacturers now offer complete lighting systems. One no longer has to build light fixtures.

Q. My reef tank has been set up for six months now and I am looking to replace my lights. I talked with John Burleson a couple of weeks ago and was told I needed two 140 watt V.H.O. Actinics and two V.H.O. Daylights, the Daylight bulb's number being F60 T12/D V.H.O. I've tried locally and through some of the advertisers in the magazine, and none can find a listing of this bulb. I also just finished your article in November's FAMA saying how the H.O. gave a greater intensity of U.V. light. Would the H.O. and V.H.O. bulbs still be the better choice? If so, do you know any suppliers from which I would obtain these bulbs and the U.V. lens you used? My tank is 62" long so I would like to have the 60" bulb for full coverage.

Any help you could provide would be greatly appreciated. Keep up the excellent work in your column. I really enjoy how your column is geared more towards the experienced hobbyist. Sincerely, Jeff Joos, Kettering, OH

Hardware stores generally carry daylight bulbs. Aquarium Industry manufacturers offer a wide array of full spectrum daylight and/or actinic combinations that can be purchased from your pet dealer.

A. John's recommendation is right on, and would give you excellent results. The five foot V.H.O. Daylight can be a bit tricky to find, as you noted. I suggest that you look up Sylvania or Philips dealers in your yellow pages if you haven't done so already. You might also try calling these companies directly, explaining your situation, in order to find out who carries these bulbs in your area. There is a four foot V.H.O. Daylight 110 watt which may be easier for you to find, but I understand your desire to have a full length bulb, and I concur with it. There are many manufacturers of Daylight bulbs, the name referring to a particular spectrum, not a general description. There are slight differences in intensity and spectra from one company to the next, and these can affect one's results. The Sylvania Daylight is the most common one used by hobbyists, though the spectral chart for the Philips Daylight is essentially identical. This is why I am recommending that you try both companies, which will increase your chances of finding the bulb you seek.

Regarding the question of U.V., I will have more to say in the coming months. For now, Jeff, I recommend that you consider making your own lens using either glass or a U.V. absorbing acrylic such as Lexan. Please don't make too much out of the point I am making about U.V. light. You can have great success in your tank using the above mentioned lamps without lenses, but blocking out the ultraviolet rays emitted by the Daylight bulbs will give superior results with organisms that are either sensitive to U.V., or slow to adapt to it.* At the end of the column there is a reference which details some of the effects of U.V. on sensitive organisms, as well as its not too widely known ability to penetrate deeply into clear waters.

*I no longer consider it necessary to use lenses on fluorescent lights. Please see my comments elsewhere in this book regarding photosynthetically produced excess oxygen.

Q. I have some questions concerning the small reef tank that I have been setting up over the past four months. It is a 29 gallon tank filtered by an Aquareef USA trickle filter (the one designed for a 55 gallon tank), and a small protein skimmer. The light canopy consists of one 100 watt Metal Halide lamp and two 20 watt Actinic 03 bulbs. After I had cycled the filter with ammonium chloride, I ordered two boxes of live rock from Florida Bay Brand. When the rock arrived, I shook it vigorously in saltwater and cleaned off any obviously dead material. Then I put it in my tank and carefully monitored the ammonia and nitrite for the next month. During this time, I siphoned off the decaying matter daily.

After the "breaking" in period had completed, I decided to see what would grow out of the rocks, so I refrained from adding any animals. More importantly, I wanted to see if any harmful creatures were hiding in the rock. Since the only animals in the tank were some green sea mat, various tube worms and small "snail-like" animals, I tried putting a small piece of shrimp in the tank to see what would be drawn out. Well nothing happened so I figured that I was safe.

Still, I decided to go slowly. The zoanthids on the live rock have done well, and some Florida false coral is beginning to grow back. Finally, I added a Pink tipped anemone and a coral banded shrimp. I chose these invertebrates because they are inexpensive and would serve as good trial animals before I start adding corals and more exotic anemones.

Well, now for my problem. Although everything seems to be doing fine (water quality and animal health is good), I have discovered and removed two bristle worms that were crawling in some holes in the rock. How are you supposed to clean them from the fresh live rock if they are deep inside? Also every once in a while, something seems to spit a puff of sand out of the live rock — I guest something is burrowing (the bristle worms?). And finally, I have noticed some long "tentacles" coming out of the rock, mostly but not always at night, apparently searching for food. Are reef aquariums always going to have a few bristle worms, and if they are detrimental to the reef tank, how can I get rid of them? Or are they, perhaps, a non-destructive species? And are the "burrowing animals" and the "tentacles" similarly dangerous to the tank? Why would it have taken since June for these things to show up? I had wanted to order some seeded decorator rock, some soft corals, and some anemones from Aquatic Specialists in Knoxville, Tennessee, but I don't want to put anything in if they are going to be destroyed. Are things going normally, or should I be worried? Thank you, Bill Darr, Columbia, South Carolina

A. I don't think that I can do much about you being worried, but I'll certainly try. Don't sweat it, Bill, there's nothing wrong with being methodical, and I admire your patience and observational skills.

Now, as to why you are noticing bristle worms suddenly, I suspect that you neglected to mention that you have a fair amount of sand or gravel on the bottom of the tank. While it is nothing out of the ordinary to find an occasional bristle worm, I have noticed that they really proliferate when there is gravel present — just an observation. They (some types) are detrimental to the tank, so they should be removed. Bristle worms, most notably the giant *Hermodice carunculata*, will eat away at corals and anemones, and are often the reason why one's anemone seems to have lost some tentacles. The other critters you noticed are not harmful, and I will describe them shortly. You can lure and retrieve bristle worms by placing some shrimp in a nylon bag or the end of a stocking, tying it closed and attaching a long string or monofilament that can be draped over the wall of the aquarium in order to allow easy retrieval. The bag should be left on the bottom of the aquarium only overnight when the lights are out, and retrieved in the morning. If there are many bristle worms in the tank, they will be swarming around the bag, and will be easy to remove.*

*Worm traps are also now available from your pet dealer. See the article about bristle worms by Dr. Ron Shimek, in the Summer 1994 issue of *Aquarium Frontiers* journal.

There are many organisms which actually bore through the live rock, but most of the "puffs" you've observed belong to worms that are deposit or detritus feeders. The tentacles you observed belong to a critter known to those who are scientifically inclined as a terebellid worm or *Amphitrite*. To the layman they are known as spaghetti worms. The puffs of sand and detritus are not a result of the animal's burrowing, but are, instead, the concentrated waste from all of the food it has collected from the surrounding rocks and plants with its far reaching tentacles. Some of these worms eject their waste violently into the water, benefitting those filter feeding organisms which reside downstream. Others merely let the waste flow out of their crevice in the rock, creating grey detritus heaps.

Spaghetti worms are fascinating to watch as they reel in their food, their tentacles like so many conveyor belts. If memory serves me correctly, they have three methods of food retrieval, depending on particle size. The smallest particles move by means of ciliary currents along a central groove on the tentacle, hence the appearance that they are gliding along. Larger particles are pulled in by muscular contractions along the length of the tentacle, and really big mouthfuls are wrapped by a tentacle and reeled in. The worm feeds on bacteria and microorganisms living on these particles. The only annoying feature of spaghetti worms is the detritus piles, though often the concentration makes clean-up by siphoning easier. No worries, mate!

Q. I live in Australia and as yet the aquarium trade is not as advanced as in the U.S. This is slowly changing with two aquariums here in Sydney starting to make dry/wet filters, but from what I have read in FAMA, they are still doing it the old way with calcite in the wet filter. I would like to change my current dry/wet filter to one with a foam cartridge in the wet section — is this necessary or not? As can be seen from my sketch I need to put the foam where shown so I do not have to shut the system down to change the design of it. This cartridge would be large, and after reading the June 1989 issue of FAMA, I was wondering if it would be too much of a drain on the oxygen in the tank. If so, how can I rectify that without putting an airstone inside the tank. Any other suggestions would be welcome. I have a protein skimmer on my tank. Are they good for mini-reef set-ups and should they be used continuously or intermittently? I am confused as to what I should use to maintain pH. Thank you, Mick Garland, Sydney, Australia

The foam block could go here instead. (see text)

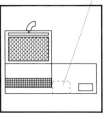

I no longer recommend a foam block in the sump, so this answer serves merely to show the change in my opinion since I wrote the column.

A. Looking at your sketch I see a better alternative for foam placement. Before I get into that I want to state again that this foam serves primarily as a particulate filter before the pump, catching the sloughed off bacterial slime that continuously rains down from the dry section. It also serves a minor biological function, but this is insignificant compared with the function of the dry filter and living rock. In other words, it's up to you whether you want to have the sponge there at all. Instead of putting the foam block directly under the dry section, you could place it in front of the center partition wall in the sump, and support it there by means of a custom cut piece of eggcrate grid. This would give you much easier access to it. You could also use another piece of eggcrate to hold in activated carbon or other chemical filter media. A large foam block would remove oxygen from the water, but this would have little negative effect on the system unless it was left to clog for a long period.

I have talked about protein skimming in a previous column, so I will restrict my comments to stating simply that I consider it an important aid in reef keeping, and I do run mine continuously. If you find that your skimmer stops working after a while, generally there are three possible reasons why, and the commonly held notion that there is nothing left to skim is not one of them. Either the column has accumulated deposits of foam-breaking compounds and needs to be cleaned, or you are using enough ozone to prevent skimming, or it is simply time to replace the airstone.* Constantly putting ones hands in the tank also impedes skimming because of the introduction of oils from the skin which make the foam collapse.

*or it is time to clean dust and salt from the clogged venturi orifice.

pH control in the reef tank is a subject misunderstood by many new reef keepers who previously kept freshwater fish or saltwater fish-only tanks. In the latter two, one tests the pH periodically to assess whether it has changed due to the processes of nitrification and organic accumulation, and takes steps to correct the pH if it is above or below what it should be. The difference with reef tanks is that the pH value is often more dynamic than in fish-only systems. It is perfectly normal for a reef tank to have a pH range from 8.0 to 8.4 within a twenty four hour period. Larger tanks tend to be more stable than this, and heavily planted tanks (lots of algae) may show even greater swings. When a reef keeping hobbyist tells me the pH of his tank is ... I immediately ask what time of day he took this value, and whether he has tested it at other times of the day. It is not unusual either for the value to be fairly constant in the water, and this will depend in part on the amount of buffer in solution and population in the tank. So, what to do? I generally only check the carbonate hardness of my water to assess the range of pH I can expect. I seldom check the pH. About once a month I find that the hardness has fallen enough that I need to add some Kh booster. As I have mentioned before in this column, I keep my tanks at natural full strength seawater conditions: Salinity 1.025, Kh 7-8dKh. Still, I must emphasize the fact that other hobbyists have success at much lower salinity's, often with a higher carbonate hardness.**

**My answer here neglects the very important use of kalkwasser to maintain pH, alkalinity and calcium. This is discussed in later columns.

I will end this month's column in a different manner. I have a question for you this time. I'd like to hear back from you or at least get you thinking on this one.

Q. Why is it that most reef keeping hobbyists are men? Never mind all the wives and girlfriends who patiently put up with the insanity of owning a reef, and often do their share of work on it ... just tell me why you think this is mostly a man's hobby? I'll be looking forward to your responses.

References Jokiel, P.L. 1980. *Solar Ultraviolet Radiation and Coral Reef Epifauna.* Science, Vol. 207, 7 March 1980. pp 1069-1071.

April 1990

Q. I have a 150 gallon saltwater fish tank. I am planning to change it to an invertebrate reef tank. My tank has three openings at the bottom that connect to the intake of my pump, filtration, heater, and U.V. lighting. If I install a reef filter, I would like to know the following: (please see sketch enclosed).

150 gallon saltwater fish tank.

Note: **This is not a recommended configuration! Please read criticisms in text.**

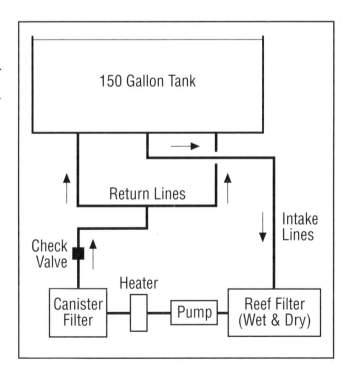

(1) Can I still use these three openings at the bottom of my tank? (Two for return and one for intake to the new reef filter.)

(2) The actual pump I am using is a March Ac-4c-MD; can I still re-use this pump to return the water to the tank without having problems due to the increase in temperature because of the use of this pump?

(3) The actual canister filter is made by Aquanetics. Model #130. Can I still re-use it and install it after the reef and pump to filter the water better?

Thank you very much for your time and assistance. Sincerely, Ivan Fernandez, Fremont, CA

A. I have been asked the very same question(s) many times, owing to the change of late from old state of the art in reverse-flow canister systems, to new state of the art in wet/dry filtered systems. Your letter brings up some interesting points I want to discuss, but first of all I want to answer your questions.

Yes you can still use the three openings, though I have some important modifications to your plans. The March pump will work fine, and I don't expect a temperature problem in a 150 gallon tank, but if you have noticed such a problem before, you might need to ventilate the cabinet or choose an alternate pump. To achieve greater water velocity in your tank, you might consider a stronger pump. In your previous arrangement the pump was sending fluid in a closed system without working against "head" or water column due to gravity. In your new plans the pump would be working against both water column and the pleated cartridge or mechanical filter in the canister. This will reduce its output a bit, and splitting the return will further decrease the velocity of the water entering the tank, with the end result being a reef tank with inadequate water motion. I have seen many aquaria running with fine water turnover through the filter, but poor circulation within the aquarium. You should plan to install a pump that will feed the maximum that your filter can handle draining down. In choosing or designing a filter, you should keep in mind the pump output needed to generate good circulation. The theoretical, "not to be exceeded" perfect flow rate for optimal biological filtration in a reef tank is, in my opinion, so much theoretical salt creep. In a fish-only system, I can see that an optimal flow through the filter could be demonstrated, but in a reef tank we have the tremendous biological surface in live rock substrates, so the optimal effect is achieved when the water really moves.

I can understand your wanting to salvage everything from your old system, but to give you my honest opinion I think I must step on a few toes. I see no real benefit in having such post-filtration, and I see a real disadvantage in utilizing a pleated cartridge here. The cartridge will lower the output of the pump, as stated earlier, and will eventually need cleaning — an added maintenance chore with no complementary benefit to the system. A foam cartridge in the wet section (sump) of the wet/dry filter catches the bacteria-generated detritus, and is easier to service. The heater may also be located in the sump, though negligent hobbyists who don't have automatic water top-off systems to make up for water lost to evaporation have been rudely awakened to the fact that heaters must remain submerged! So you may wish to continue using your heater module. If you wish to employ the canister for chemical filtration, that would be fine though, again, locating this media in the sump makes for easier servicing.

Finally, I want to comment on some necessary modifications to your plans. I know it was simply an oversight that you did not include the extension (partition) to the surface for your "intake line" or drain to the filter. Without it, of course, the whole tank would drain onto the floor. Since the hole is in the middle of the tank, you may either build a partition around it (perhaps an awkward location for servicing or decorating, or an ideal one to build the reef around), or plug the hole and drill a new one either in a back corner or somewhere along the back of the tank. Wherever you locate the drain hole, you must install a solid partition for surface skimming, concealment of the prefilter, and to be sure to avoid draining the whole tank. The standpipe in this partitioned area should be perforated to allow air to escape as water drains down. Since you have planned two returns, one could be used as a bottom return and the other for the surface. The check valve in your diagram ought to be a very good one if you wish to have a bottom return ... a failure with this one part could make you a very unpopular guy!*

*I no longer recommend check valves. More specifically, I recommend avoiding any plumbing design that requires a check valve to prevent water from draining down. After years of experience with them I have come to accept Julian's variation on Murphy's law: "check valves always fail eventually."

Another possibility deserves brief mention. Although I have not tried the idea, it is possible to run a closed, pressurized trickle system using canisters and an air pump, and this could be installed to use the holes you have, without the need for a partition, though you might extend a pipe up for surface extraction. In this system, a pleated cartridge would serve as prefilter. As this is a closed system, you have the advantages of reduced water evaporation and virtually no "head" due to water column for the pump to work against. Also, a pressurized trickle filter is supposed to work more efficiently in theory, at least. One such system is advertised in this magazine.

A number of hobbyists have asked me about installing post filters on their reef tanks, complaining of cloudy water and asserting the need to polish it clear. In my experience, cloudy water in the reef tank is indicative of a biological imbalance, and mechanical filtration is not the solution. If this problem exists, there may be fouling organism(s), or the bottom substrate may be too thick, especially in newly established reef tanks. Often the problem occurs in reef tanks with poor circulation. Increasing the velocity of water flow in the tank frequently solves the problem by providing better penetration of oxygen rich water throughout all the substrates, including the rock, thus encouraging the growth of beneficial microorganisms. If the problem persists despite these corrections, a chemical imbalance of the buffering system might exist, though this would be unlikely. A water change would be the solution, assuming the source of water is not the source of the problem. Cloudiness in a newly established reef tank is not unusual, and can be solved by the addition of some old seeded live rock (been in someone's tank so long he can't remember) and the addition of Aquarium Products' Biozyme. Both of these boost the population of heterotrophic organisms needed to get the tank back in balance.

One more item concerning your question should be discussed. Though you didn't ask me, one might reasonably ask about continuing to use the reverse flow undergravel filter. There are some disadvantages to using reverse flow filtration on a reef tank. While such filtration would virtually eliminate the formation of anaerobic areas in the gravel, the passage of the filtered water through the bottom media would lower the dissolved oxygen level in the tank, though not especially worse than the passage of water through gravel in a "wet filter." Having experienced the clean results in a fish-only exhibit using reverse flow, one might reasonably assume that the upward flow through the gravel would prevent the accumulation of detritus there. Unfortunately, the relatively slow velocity of water coming up through the gravel does not prevent the heavy detritus accumulations that occur with live rock. Finally, reef systems using undergravel filtration of any kind tend to develop heavy populations of undesirable bristle worms.* As always, it is possible to have excellent success with many organisms using the systems I don't recommend, though I do my best to offer experience that tends to support or justify my recommendations.

*The small bristle worms that live in the gravel may be unsightly, but they are generally harmless scavengers that benefit the system by aerating the gravel with their movements and eating detritus.

Q. I have a 55 gallon invertebrate tank. On 11/2/89 I took off my metal halide 175 watt and put on four 18" Actinic 03 30 watt and two 30 watt Ultralume 50. The way my tank is constructed, I can only put on three foot long bulbs. I put two Actinics and one Ultralume under one reflector, the same in the other reflector. The two Actinics run in a straight line next to the three foot bulb. I have tried Elegance coral and *Goniopora* under the metal halide and both started to shrink after only one week. On 11/3/89, I decided to give the Elegance and *Goniopora* one more try. I put both in the tank on the evening of 11/3/89 and I am happy to report that as I am writing this letter, both have increased in size and they really look beautiful. One problem I have in my tank is that I have an abundance of *Anemonia anemonia* growing in my tank that are having some effect on some of my corals. My tank houses: Elegance coral, *Goniopora,* multiple mushrooms, three different types of leather coral, two types of button coral, small feather dusters that are multiplying, bubble coral, cleaner shrimp, sponges that are growing (blue), cleaner wrasse, flame angel, kole tang, cardinal fish, watchman goby, two baby starfish, brittlestars, and plenty of limpets. I hope that you have an answer for my *Anemonia anemonia* problem. Sincerely, Fred T. Hutter Blue Bell, PA

A. *Aiptasia* you have, Fred, not *Anemonia*. These little anemones can be a real pest, as you've noticed, since they do harm many prized specimens, including corals and *Tridacna* clams, and multiply like mad. You may have noticed that smushing and mutilating these beasts does no good ... they always recover, sometimes multiply in response. If they happen to stray onto the glass, however, they can be removed with a razor blade and small siphon. When they multiply on the rocks, however, they are more difficult to eradicate. Wilkens recommends the copperband butterfly, *Chelmon rostratus*, for biological control, but that fish will also decimate your feather dusters. Other butterflies will also eat the *Aiptasia,* but may try your corals as well. All-out warfare can be waged by injecting the anemones with potassium chloride using a hypodermic needle. I have seen no other recommendations for getting rid of them.*

*Future columns discuss the use of boiling water, calcium hydroxide, potassium hydroxide, and Racoon butterflies. More recently the discovery that certain corals sting and kill Aiptasia *has offered perhaps the best cure of all. See appendix.*

I feel I must comment on your lighting and observations. I think that the time periods you gave may be too brief to make any definite conclusions about the corals' health, though truthfully, detrimental and beneficial effects of lighting often are manifest in just a few days. I am pretty certain that you are using the wrong ballasts for the Actinic 30 watt bulbs. It's just a hunch, but I bet you're using three double 30 watt ballasts to run all six bulbs. You should be using two double 60 watt high output ballasts for the Actinics since they are high output bulbs, and a double 30 watt ballast for the Ultralumes. Forgive me for making the accusation if you are doing it correctly, and forgive me everyone for running this matter into the ground, but the mistake is too easily and too often made. Now, if my hunch is correct, I have still one more recommendation for you. You might try 24" 40 watt high output. Actinics instead of the 18" 30 watt bulbs. These would also use a 60 watt high output ballast. Perhaps you decided to use the 18" bulbs for space reasons, I don't know, but if you could sandwich the

Ultralumes™, each between two 24" Actinics, you would have a big more intensity; and better results. The two-foot bulbs would be staggered for even distribution of the light.

Q. I've had my 29 gallon reef tank set up for nine months and just recently have I been adding fish, corals, and anemones. There are nine fish which include a pair of mandarins, a pair of percula clowns, one purple *Pseudochromis*, one canary blenny, one seahorse, and one yellow jawfish. The invertebrates consist of two feather dusters, one coral banded shrimp, one orange sponge, one yellow polyp, one Elegance coral, one cup coral, one cauliflower coral, one finger coral, one *Euphyllia,* and one bubble coral. Everything is doing fine but I cannot keep any anemones for longer than four weeks. After two weeks, the anemone shrinks and turns itself inside out by pushing its insides out through its mouth. My system is made up of an overflow corner, wet/dry filter and a protein skimmer. The lights consist of one 24" Actinic 03, two 24" Ultralumes™, and one Vitalite™. The pH is 8.3. The nitrite, nitrate, and ammonia levels are zero, with a carbonate hardness of 14. I feed twice a week with CoralLife® Target food and hand feed with silversides. No one can tell me what's wrong. Thanks, Mark Ensminger, Enolia, PA

A. In one of my earlier columns I covered the "trouble with anemones" subject, but let's look at it again since no one could offer Mark any help.

The rigors of shipping often prove too much for anemones, and many of them die within a couple of weeks from injuries received in shipping and handling, even though they may initially appear to have recovered. As I said before, anemones generally fare best when shipped without water covering them. Large anemones tend to suffocate when shipped in water, as they consume all the dissolved oxygen. Such anemones typically have the inverted "jelly doughnut" appearance, something like what you are seeing in your dying anemones

... an important observation. Anemones will exhibit this behavior at extremes of oxygen concentration. The hyperoxic condition — too high a concentration of dissolved oxygen — is not indicated in your system, and is unlikely in any aquarium, except under tow circumstances: (1) very intense lighting combined with no water movement, in which case the oxygen concentration within the tissues of the anemone can be too high as result of photosynthetic zooxanthellae (Dykens and Shick, 1983), and (2) the injection of pure oxygen into an evacuated, pressurized trickling column (an "oxygen reactor") ... (John Burleson, pers. comm.). I think "ozone reactor" would be a more appropriate name since ozone is safely used in these.

A hypo-oxic condition, too little dissolved oxygen within the tissues, can occur again when there is little or no water movement around the anemone. This might be a factor in your anemone losses.

Note: Trace element additions are also important for anemones. They may assist in the development of pigments, and seem to help with preventing the buildup of excess oxygen from photosynthesis.

Two other considerations affect your success with anemones, Mark, and these are lighting and food. You could have success with anemones in a 29 gallon tank with the lighting you have now, but your chances would be much improved if you would have at least two of the 24" tubes be high output bulbs, necessitating the purchase of a high output ballast. I can tell you for certain that you are feeding the anemones too much, especially considering the lighting you have. Since the symbiotic zooxanthellae consume waste ammonia from their anemone host, the more intense the light, the more food (protein) the anemone can handle. In general, most people who successfully maintain anemones find that they need not be fed much at all. A spectrum of opinion ranges from no feeding whatsoever to the occasional morsel of food. I advise you to do away with the silversides altogether. Ultimately, you will work out a routine of feeding or not feeding your anemones.

Finally, as I have warned before, beware the bristle worm, for he may munch away and kill your helpless anemone.

Q. I have just recently started a 70 gallon reef tank. It seems all to be going well. I have purchased two boxes of Indo live rock to start my reef, about 70-80 lbs. Three weeks after I put the rock in the tank I noticed these two small critters going about their business. Enclosed is a small drawing and description of these things I observed in my tank. I would like to know if anyone at FAMA has come across these things before, and are they good news or bad news? Thank you, Richard Vieco, Flushing, NY

A. Well, aside from the terrible end for fish that your town forebodes, I have pretty good news for you. The critters you describe are common and harmless. I don't know if the kind and talented staff at FAMA can print your drawings, so I have included your written descriptions for the benefit of the readers.

Monster number one: *"This looks like a brine shrimp with short legs, but it burrows and acts like a small ant and makes little burrows at, and above, the sand level."*

Monster number two: *"Body color clear pink. The `V' tail sticks to glass and the head seems to be off glass and sways and can move about slowly. Uses head to move."*

Let's start with the second critter since your description and drawing leave me confident in its identification as a tiny herbivorous flatworm. These can really multiply in a reef aquarium, and some hobbyists consider them a nuisance, but I have never seen any harm done by them. There are many beautiful flatworms that can be introduced with live rock. Most present no risk to the inhabitants, but a few are specialized parasites and can be a problem. The pinkish type you refer to I have seen with Indonesian coral specimens, and it appears to be colored to blend with the crustose coralline algae on the rocks. Only on the glass, where they multiply feeding on the film of diatoms, are they conspicuous. Another cryptic little flatworm has the same outline as the one you described, "V" tail and rounded head, but blends perfectly with the color and surface of the mushroom anemones that it preys upon (Wilkens, 1987). You will have to look very carefully to spot these and, fortunately, they are not common.

There are a few different "bugs" that roughly fit the first description, but experience tells me that you are probably noticing amphipods, though your drawing suggests a miniature stomatopod (mantis shrimp). Amphipods are laterally compressed and most of the common ones in our tanks look very much like fleas. Hobbyists often describe them as shrimp-like, for the lack of a better comparison. Although they may straighten out when on the move, a good characteristic for identification is that they have a curved back, like a flea. Still, there are numerous species that have evolved into some very bizarre-looking shapes indeed. The "skeleton shrimp," or Caprellid, is just one of these that might occur in our aquaria. Most amphipods encountered in the aquarium are herbivores and detritivores, which means that they are very desirable for algae control and digestion of detritus. In addition, since they multiply rapidly and are tasty and nutritious, your fish will benefit by their presence. Some fish, such as mandarins and wrasse, are capable of depleting amphipod numbers significantly as they browse about the live rock. Interestingly, the gravel bed does provide the best breeding ground for amphipods, and mandarinfish can be maintained indefinitely without feeding when there is sufficient gravel to prevent them from completely decimating the amphipod population, as they may in a small aquarium without bottom media. I guess after all the negative press I've given gravel in the reef aquarium, I had to throw in a token benefit.

I have seen a tiny species of mantis shrimp that fits your description, and it, too, is harmless, beneficial, and good fish food. Larger species of mantis shrimp are "bad news," and you should read past columns to find out how to get rid of them. I doubt that the critters you are seeing are babies of a large species.

Other shrimp-like creatures you might see include copepods, isopods, and mysiid shrimp. If you want to see copepods, take a look at the lower corners of your tank. On the glass you will notice minute specs that usually move about in a jerky fashion. The common species are whitish and have a pair of antennae and tail filaments. They are mostly benthic, but will occasionally jump off the substrate and swim. Typically you will notice many "couples" stuck together, and some females with twin egg bundles. Some copepods are highly specialized parasites, but these are not commonly encountered in the aquarium. For the most part, the copepods you see in a reef tank eat algae and detritus, and are an excellent supplemental food for both fish and invertebrates. Many are commensals on the invertebrates, and many are important in the consumption of decaying matter.

Mysiid shrimp, also known as oppossum shrimp, look very much like Euphasiids or "krill." They are not common in most wet/dry filtered reef tanks, but some lucky or skilled hobbyists have them. They have been cultured for years in Europe as fish food, and can multiply sufficiently in the reef tank to serve as a perpetual food source for the fish. Seahorses love them. I have only noticed two species that multiply in reef aquaria. One is so small it is easily mistaken for a copepod, though the smooth gliding motion and characteristic mysiid shape distinguish it to the unaided eye. The other attains a size of roughly 3/8 of an inch and has some red pigment in the body. Both appear to subsist on algae-generated detritus, though it is possible that they also prey on copepods.

Remember the "roley poley" bugs you used to find crawling about the garden when you were a kid? You know, they would roll up like tiny armadillos. Well, they were isopods. There are lots of them in your reef tank, believe me, and some species can play an important role in making your tank look better than Joe's, since, like the amphipods, many isopods are little algae grazers. The appearance of the isopods in your reef can range from long-legged critters that look and scurry around like house centipedes (which are completely unrelated), to large, black-eyed bugs that swim so fast you can't believe it. Some of them are blood-sucking fish parasites, such as *Renocila heterozota*, but these are large, conspicuous, and very rarely encountered in the aquarium, though they are common on the reef.

I'll never forget the giant isopods we netted from deep water in the Straits of Florida during a summer cruise when I was in the marine biology course at the University of Florida. Talk about childhood nightmare come to life ... imagine a "roley poley" as big as your

Reebocks, with shiny black eyes and huge crushing mandibles! Word has it they're good eatin' too ... as good as lobster. And what was I thinking as I picked up one of these beasties, which happened to be carrying a clutch of babies each the size of a walnut? — if only I could keep one alive in an aquarium, of course!

References

Dykens, J.A. and J.M. Shick. 1983. Protection Against Photosynthetic Oxygen by Animals Containing Endosymbiotic Algae. Am. Zool. 24:978.

Wilkens, P. and J. Birkholtz. 1987. *Niedere Tiere. Steinkorallen Scheiben-Und Krusten Anemonen.* Engelbert Pfriem Verlag, Wuppertal.

May 1990

To start this month's column off, I want to re-emphasize the big three: Temperature, Light, and Water Motion. If you haven't got these down, ain't no piece of fancy equipment gonna save your anemone, mate! Take control of nutrients, and take care of proper placement — orientation and room. That's about all you need for a successful living reef aquarium. Anything else is only a matter of convenience and luxury. Oh yeah, a bit of aesthetic judgment and a whole lot of experience can help, too!

In keeping with my intention of thoughtfully and open-mindedly providing you with the latest practical information, I must regress a bit and present a couple of alternative points of view. Really, when I get letters like these it does not make my day, but don't let that stop you. I'd rather hear your gripe, if you've got one, than not hear from you at all.

Dear FAMA, (Re: Nov. '89 Reef Notes)

I have been keeping a 60 gallon reef tank containing some five different species of corals without fatalities (among these invertebrates, at least) for over two years. For the last year and a half, I have been using metal halide lighting. So imagine my surprise when I discovered in reading in your article that this type of lighting is "poisonous" to corals!

This illustrates a very common phenomenon. Someone does an "experiment," gets the result they were looking for, and tries to cast it as his or her own unique discovery of one of nature's laws, totally ignoring myriads of other variables. The reef-keeping hobby will not flourish without a more responsible approach than this.

Your "Photo #4" shows a group of fungus corals very similar to one I have in my tank that has been doing very well under this "poisonous" lighting for some time now. (I didn't knowingly introduce this specimen, it just sprung out of one of the rocks.) At one time, however, it nearly died. This was possibly because it was too close to the light, like the ones in the photo. (Take strong note of my use of the word "possibly," and please consider making more liberal use of it.) It began to flourish when I moved it closer to the bottom of the tank. It is nearly 6" across now, and attaining the characteristic greenish tinge of the symbiotic algae living in the tissue of a healthy specimen.

It would be simple-minded to believe that the only variable that changes with water depth is light intensity. The only real fact of the matter is that in my case, this particular specimen became happier when positioned closer to the bottom of my tank. Period. Further conclusions would be completely invalid without some very intricate testing. Why do people insist in making these ludicrous assumptions about light?

I also have a species of "Hammerhead" coral, generally considered to be one of the most difficult types of keep, less than 6" from the metal halide fixture! In spite of enduring this heavy dose of poison for two years now, it continues to thrive. I will send photos when I finally figure out how to get the correct exposures under this type of lighting. (I noticed you also had a bit of difficulty with this.)

No I do not work for a lighting company. Furthermore, I do not, like so many hobbyists, defend a particular technology to the death merely because I have invested in it myself, and do not want to admit the mistake, nor deny its value completely because I could not afford it at the time. I am beginning to suspect that these are major fac-

The harmful effect was not from any particular wavelength, but from photosynthetically produced excess oxygen in the tissues. One might wonder how metal halide intensity differs from sunlight in the ability to produce a "toxic" effect from photosynthesis, considering the much greater intensity of natural sunlight. The difference has to do with clouds. Clouds offer pauses in photosynthesis that allow the animal to detoxify or get rid of the excess oxygen. The light in the aquarium is constant, and when intense beyond a threshold level it produces the effect described. Trace elements also help the animal to deal with the excess oxygen.

tors in some of the "theories." (Not to mention theories produced by those who work for manufacturers!)
Mr. Sprung's dissertation about the infra-red and far red wavelengths were reminiscent of George C. Scott's role in the movie, "Doctor Strangelove," in which he spoke of the "communist plot of flouridization." At exactly what wavelength, in Mr. Sprung's view, do these insidious spectra exist? Why "infra-red," and not ultraviolet? And what instrumentation was used in order to arrive at this surprising conclusion? And whatever is the "harmful effect" that this wavelength has on these creatures?* Sunburn? Psoriasis? And are these spectra not present in abundance in natural sunlight? The last time I checked, sunlight was rather rich in the infra-red spectrum. It is naive to believe that even the most powerful metal halides could begin to approach its intensity.

If I had to guess, I would say that the shift in health of the creatures in Mr. Gutierrez' tank was due to a change in some other maintenance habit, likely feeding.

Please remember that there are beginners out there, making purchasing decisions based on this stuff, before making this rather rash type of statement. I personally have been burned once or twice by believing statements like this, perhaps more than any invertebrate will ever be burned by a metal halide lamp! Please, for the sake of the hobby, let's drop this witch-hunt approach to lighting once and for all, and stick to the facts. Sincerely, Chris Doole, Manitoba, Canada

Dear Don,
I am writing this letter in reference to statements made by one of your contributing editors, Mr. Julian Sprung, in his recent column entitled, "Reef Notes" pertaining to metal halide lighting and the negative effects that it has on reef animals.

While I have a great deal of respect for the knowledge that Mr. Sprung has accumulated over the years, I feel that a lot of his statements about metal halide lighting in both your magazine and other hobbyist magazines in the field, are erroneous and misleading to the average home hobbyist who wishes to maintain a so-called "mini-reef type set-up." Anyone who is familiar with my work and subsequent experimentation with all sources of lighting dating back to the early 1980's and to present date, knows my particular views on metal halide lighting versus actinic lighting. Some hobbyists and professionals might be familiar with the experiments I carried out during the year 1988 and, which was printed and documented in Mr. Thiel's Marine Reef Newsletter, Volume II, #19, wherein, I subjected various reef animals to both metal halide and actinic lighting. In addition, various Macroalgae of both *Caulerpa* sp. and *Halimeda* sp. were also included in the experiments. Being first and foremost a medical physician, specifically a pathologist who is Board Certified in both anatomic pathology and clinical chemistry, I have access to some pretty sophisticated laboratory instrumentation whereby I closely monitored for a period of one year, various invertebrate species in two separate tanks with two different lighting set-ups. Since I was able to test, and have documented such in marine reef, all pertinent water parameters from ammonia on through to dissolved oxygen, iron, calcium, heavy metals, etc., and since I used a high grade of reagent deionized water and the same salt mix, I was only able to conclude and present my findings to other fellow marine aquarists based on proper scientific method. It is quite evident that anyone who read my column in the "Marine Reef Newsletter," could clearly see that more species of marine invertebrates and algae not only survived and did much better under halide lighting, but also increased in size and reproduced in a captive tank situation without supplementary feeding. Clearly, the metal halide lighting provided proper photosynthetic processes by the zooxanthellae algae within the invertebrate tissues. Furthermore, I presented a brief summary of metal halide lighting as compared to actinic lighting and I made some pertinent points about the erroneous statements made by certain people in the industry and/or hobby who claim that hard corals burn under metal halide lighting. In reality, in my experience, in which I might add is backed up by a lot of experience from other scientists and aquarists who strive to maintain hard corals and invertebrate animals in closed environments, that metal halide light has clearly provided a source of photosynthetic bands and intense light that cannot only maintain hard coral and various anemone species but very closely simulates the intensity and the natural spectra of sunlight.

I find it rather interesting that Mr. Sprung was at one time affiliated with Sea Kleer Reefs, Inc. who counted itself as the original actinic light specialist. This same company has now procured the exclusive distributorship of a well-known German Company who exclusively deals in and introduced metal halide lighting to the industry both here in the United States and Canada. If actinic lighting was the "end-all and be-all" of aquarium lighting, then, why now, metal halide lights? Furthermore, I think that there ought to be more scientific and documented research printed in fine publications such as your own, in order to clear up and further advance both the industry and the hobby rather than erroneous statements with limited scientific experimentation and lack of reproducibility from one tank to the next. I know several people both in the hobby and in the scientific field who have since switched to metal halide lighting and have found it to be more than satisfactory for maintenance of the majority of invertebrate animals currently kept at both the professional aquarium and home hobbyist level. One of the real problems with this industry and hobby is that there is a lack of adequate scientific scrutiny and certain individuals who only seek to set themselves up as the "expert," can produce results that have neither been scientifically documented nor have been able to be reproduced.

I caution my fellow hobbyists that before they jump on the mini-reef bandwagon, that they do a lot of research into the qualifications of certain people in the industry who are currently producing and/or writing about certain products that supposedly are miracle workers in all aspects of the field. I certainly mean no disrespect in any of this, but being a director of a laboratory and an advanced marine aquarist, I am sincerely concerned about the lack of scientific reproducibility that is applied to the hobby end of the industry. I feel a lot of people, through no fault of their own or through misinformation or misguided intentions, have left the hobby and will continue to leave the hobby, unless adequate documentation and adequate production of fine quality products continues to address the demand and the expanse of the aquarium industry. Also, I find it both rather amusing and bewildering that certain figures who have gained prominence over the past few years with the mini-reef concept, have a limited scientific background and knowledge and yet are able to espouse their beliefs and/or personal biases through the pages of your magazine.

All I am asking for is for fairness for people who might be wanting to expand their interests in the marine side of the hobby, and specifically mini-reef set-ups, but who lack adequate guidance in this area. Immediately, two companies that currently come to mind in the United States that I have a great deal of respect for (because of their knowledge and because of the painstaking experimentation that they have personally carried out) are both supporters and advertisers in your magazine. One is Mr. Omer Dersom of Energy Savers, and the other is Mr. Albert Thiel of Thiel Aquatech. Both of these gentlemen should receive our applause and our gratitude for the beautifully constructed lighting equipment and filtration systems that they have produced and, in addition, to the various reef supplements that they have so kindly brought to the market. Both of these men have invested a large part of both their time and finances into adequate scientific experimentation and have also, unlike other individuals, subjected their products to scrutinized testing by both myself and other individuals in the hobby and industry. Furthermore, in my opinion, Mr. Thiel stands head and shoulders above a lot of people in the industry, wherein he continually offers praise and mentions products from other companies that become available other than his own in both his "Marine Reef Newsletter" and the beautifully and painstakingly research books that he has offered.

When all the dust settles in the mini-reef arena, it will be very interesting to see what companies are still around in the next several years and will continue to produce excellent products because they really care about the animals that we maintain in our aquariums rather than just making a quick buck on a gullible and inexperienced hobbyist market.

It would be interesting to see if there are any other rebuttals and/or input to my comments that I have stated in this letter that is based on scientific documentation and not hear-say and speculation.

Until we have this in our hobby, then I am afraid that a lot of the touting for any particular product ought to be taken with a large grain of salt. In the meantime, I hope that you and your editorial staff will continue to upgrade and to bring more advanced aquarium keeping articles to the serious and advanced aquarists for which your magazine was originally formulated for. Thank you. Sincerely, Joseph F. Tavares, M.D. Directory of Laboratory Sunbury Community Hospital Sunbury, Pennsylvania

A. I have a "few" comments to make regarding the charges of these letters, and one suggestion which I hope will benefit us all. First of all, my fingers are sore from all the times I have typed, "my hypothesis" or "to each his own," "there are many ways ...," "whatever works best for you," and other such comments. These were not empty statements or an attempt to fake open-mindedness. My sole interest as author of this column is to provide information based upon my experience and research, and the research of others, so that you, the reader, may benefit and achieve the satisfaction of creating an aquarium almost as beautiful as mine!

I am a biologist, and have spent thousands of hours observing marine life in Florida, the east coast of the U.S., California, the Bahamas, the Caribbean, Hawaii, and Australia. Although I have been collecting and observing marine life for at least 17 years (having grown up with Biscayne Bay in my backyard), I have been keeping my own marine aquaria for a mere thirteen years, and living reef aquaria for eight years. In the summer of 1982 I helped build and set up a 180 gallon wet/dry filtered reef tank at a pet store in N. Miami. It was the first experience I had with these systems, and the potential I saw for improvement, as well as the creative potential, fueled my continuing experimentation.

My ideas are progressive, and I am always researching

new techniques for maintaining aquaria and breeding or propagating the species we keep. Aquariums fascinate me, not for the sake of showing off expensive turbo-charged equipment or livestock that only I have and you don't. It's the beauty and mystery of the life and ecosystem that perpetuates my fascination. Its beauty is its own reward, and no-one can soothe me with compliments if I don't like how my aquarium looks. Still, not everyone is in this hobby for the same reasons.

I have an idea that I think would benefit all those aquarists contemplating the purchase of a light source. I want these two experts to take a useful step in support of the particular lights that they favor by taking photographs of their pride and joy, and sending them to me. I will print these photographs along with my own and any others that I receive from the readers, providing everyone complies with a few simple requests. Along with the pictures, please include the type, wattage, manufacturer, and quantity of the bulbs used, as well as the photoperiod (total and per bulb if timers are used). If the tank receives any natural sunlight from a window, direct or indirect, please say so. Please indicate whether there is any glass or acrylic between the lights and tank, or any special lenses or reflectors used. It would also be helpful if everyone used the same kind of film. I am recommending Kodak 200 Gold for prints, or Kodachrome 200 for slides.* A description of the aquarium, its equipment, and as many as possible of the following water parameters only should be included: temperature, specific gravity, Kh, Nitrate, Redox potential, Key specimens should be pointed out, and their history in the aquarium described. The beauty in this idea is realized when one considers that no two aquarists will see the same thing in the photographs, and the tanks will certainly not look the same. In other words, this is not a contest, but everyone will see it that way. Assuming all the specimens are thriving, hobbyists may choose what they think looks ideal, even if yours truly doesn't agree.

I wrote the column on lighting that offended these two hobbyists, specifically because I had photographic "proof" of the conditions which had previously only been described in writing. Whether these photographs

*I now use E6 process slides, 100 ASA.

really prove anything is your decision, but let them serve
as the first demonstration of the appearance of long term
damage and rapid recovery. Please note that dramatic
recovery occurred within two days, and the only variable
changed was lighting. Also note that Santiago did not
feed these corals.*

*It *was* the light
change that effected
the recovery, but this
was not proof of any
negative quality of the
former lights. The
lower intensity of the
fluorescents brought
the rate of photosyn-
thesis below a thresh-
old level where oxygen
production exceeds
consumption or detoxi-
fication.

There is an accusation in Dr. Tavares' letter that intrigues
me. This concerns the addition Dupla metal halide lights
to the line of products sold by Sea Kleer Reefs, Inc., and
suggests that John Burleson has given up on actinic lights.
Let me assure you that Mr. Burleson of Sea Kleer Reefs
(now J.P. Burleson Inc.), did not suffer a change in his
opinions about lighting. Dupla is a very prestigious company with a most admirable product line, a perfect combination with a reputable company like Sea Kleer Reefs Inc.
The metal halide fixtures are only part of an enormous
array of Dupla products, and certainly they, alone, were
not the impetus for the union between the two companies. While I was affiliated with Sea Kleer I witnessed the
progress of Mr. Burleson's home aquaria lit by Dupla fixtures, an Energy Savers fixture, and fluorescent combinations. John personally tested these light sources under
numerous conditions and for extended periods before
making any statements about their performance.

There is nothing magic about the Actinic bulb that it
should be expected to give comparable results to another light source when used at only one tenth or less the
intensity. I have published in this column minimum fluorescent lighting combinations over standard sized aquaria. By all means one should try to exceed the intensity of
these. You cannot "overlight" an aquarium using fluorescents, even with VHO bulbs. Temperature and the proper placement of the organisms are the only limitations to
consider with higher intensity bulbs of any type.

Retailers sell a lot of standard output fluorescent bulbs
for reef tanks. Small, shallow tanks with select hardy
species will do reasonably well with a sufficient number
of these, but the vast majority of photosynthetic reef
organisms will slowly perish unless provided with sufficient intensity of light, which can only be achieved with
H.O. and V.H.O. tubes if one is using fluorescents.

I do realize that, as author of this column, I take a good deal of responsibility into my hands when I write statements that can influence the purchasing and planning made by aquarists. You must understand that my intention in discussing lighting effects and affects is only to say basically: "Hey, this can happen, I think this is why it happens, let's figure out what solutions exist." While I may easily praise a given product for its merits in aquarium keeping, to criticize a product is a delicate affair. I do try to express my opinions as thoughtfully as possible, and I think that most of you appreciate this.

As I mentioned in a previous column, a lot of readers failed to notice my discussion of the success with growing *Porites asteroides* and other corals under metal halide lights at the National Zoo in Washington. The column was not strictly one-sided. The basic message I tried to get across was that yes, indeed, metal halide light sources can give excellent results, but there are times when they don't, even when used properly, and the matter needs further research.* Most of the readers got the message. Some didn't. I should also have mentioned the beautiful and successful reef exhibit at the National Aquarium in Baltimore. It utilizes a combination of metal halide and V.H.O. actinics. I really wanted to include photographic evidence of the *Porites* and other coral in that column, to balance the negative view I was also presenting, but was unable to do so. I now have obtained some pictures of the Zoo aquarium and, while the quality is not good, I hope that they are clear enough for you to make out the details I will describe.

Photo #1 is a view from the opposite side of the aquarium that was shown in a previous "Reef Notes." One can see numerous Caribbean photosynthetic gorgonians, some *Sarcophyton* sp. leather corals, an elegance coral, bottom center, an "open brain" coral (*Trachyphyllia*), bottom right, and a Caribbean stony coral, *Dichosenia stoeksi*, large pale yellow blob, upper center. Photo #2 shows the tremendous expansion of the *Trachyphyllia* head, and if you look dead center in Photo #3, you can see a thin flat veneer of new growth coming off of the *Porites asteroides*. The gorgonians and other soft corals were thriving at all locations in the aquarium, and while

*Although I was wrong about the reason, the observation of burning was a real problem, which turned out to be caused by accumulation of oxygen in the coral tissues as a result of the more rapid rate of photosynthesis under metal halide light. The addition of trace elements seems to prevent the problem, but the reason remains mysterious. See Delbeek and Sprung's *The Reef Aquarium, Vol 1* for additional information.

The photos could not be reproduced here. Please refer to the original column in *FAMA* magazine.

the stony corals pointed out at the bottom of the aquarium were all thriving, the *Dichosenia* coral remained unnaturally pale at its location in the aquarium, higher up and directly below the lights. I will not speculate why this is the case now, because ...

It's ain't over yet. I promised that I would present the results of research that Santiago Gutierrez and I were conducting. Well the results won't be presented in "Reef Notes," sorry, but they will soon appear in this magazine in a series of articles.* The articles are not anti or pro anything, being more concerned with the nature of the relationship between coral and zooxanthellae, and the parameters of the essential forms of energy they receive. I promise this will not be a re-hashing of old doctrine. I would love to tell you about some new hypotheses and interesting experiments that even Dr. Tavares, M.D. and Mr. Doole should accept, but these are reserved for the articles. They will change the way you think about lighting ... er, um, that is if you want to change the way you think, okay?

*Please see: Gutierrez, S. & J. Sprung. "Still More On Lighting: Pt. 1" *FAMA* 15(4):136.

I want to pass along some good information to you from a fine aquarist and author, Mike Paletta. He has found that lowering the salinity of his aquarium was effective in eradicating the pesky protozoan *Helicostoma,* which suddenly attacked some of the old resident corals shortly after the addition of new ones. This is a very promising solution because of its simplicity. I hope it can be demonstrated to be effective in most cases.

Also, please refer to the excellent article Mike wrote for Sea Scope (Volume 6, Summer 1989). I wish I had mentioned it in conjunction with the column on live rock stacking techniques because Mike offers some really good additional suggestions.

Next month I'll concentrate on answering your questions. Until then, it's the end of January, it's 85 degrees out in Miami, and I'm wearing' shorts. I love it!

Q. Enclosed is a macrophotograph of one of two worms in my 135 gallon saltwater aquarium. Approximately one month before, I introduced live base rock, the source of the organisms, I presume. The two worms (each approximately 2-3 cm) have been noted in close proximity to one another, and one was observed several days later coiled on the tank wall. When the coiled worm departed, a circular deposition of eggs was noted. I have been unable to identify the worm in my library of marine invertebrates, and I was hoping that you could shed any light on the identification. Thank you, Paul LeBourgeois

A. Your description of the circular deposition of eggs on the tank wall immediately confirmed this "worm" was no worm, but, in fact, a nudibranch, a type of sea slug. When I looked at your photograph, I knew I had seen this fellow before, but I could not recall when or where. Also I must admit that you stumped me, as its name wasn't tucked away anywhere in my head ... oh, the shame of it! So, it was time to visit the library at the Rosenstiel School of Marine and Atmospheric Sciences to discover who this slug really is. Easier said than done! After browsing through several nudibranch identification texts, I had just about given up when finally I came across a drawing which matched your photo reasonably well. On that basis, let's say you might have a *Madrella sanguinea* or *Madrella* sp., though I suspect the I.D. is incorrect. If yours don't run out of food or go over the overflow, you might be able to enjoy their company for several months, perhaps years if the young survive. It is unlikely that you will enjoy them for more than a few months, though, as most nudibranchs feed on one or two species of obscure, "hard to come by" invertebrate, and merely starve in our tanks. Still there are exceptions, so good luck!

While we're on the subject of nudibranchs, some of you have asked me what I think about keeping them in a reef tank. Well, there are a few words of caution in order here. First, recall that I said that these colorful slugs have a habit of wandering over the overflow, often against their will. Aside from the injury to the specimen, or death of the specimen that results from this trip over the falls, there is another potential danger. A number of reliable hobbyists have reported to me that such misfortune for the little slug created an ever greater misfortune for the entire tank, namely the loss of most fish and some invertebrates. Certain nudibranchs contain very potent toxins which are released when they are stressed or injured. Recall that I also said that most nudibranchs have very specific diets. Many feed on only one particular species of sponge, bryozoan, or hydroid, and even if they happen to find this food growing on the live rock, they are most likely to completely consume it in a few days, and slowly starve from then on. Pity them not, though, for oddly enough they seem to retain their natural life span of several months to a year, whether they feed or not! At least this has been my personal experience. A few species of nudibranchs, and the related anaspids (sea hares) and saccoglossans, are completely herbivorous and may be bred and reared easily in an aquarium.*

*There are numerous nudibranchs which are either commensals or predators of stony and soft corals. Please see *The Reef Aquarium, Vol1* and Wilkens' and Birkholz's *Marine Invertebrates, Vol 1 and 2.* for information about these.

Q. A friend of mine gave me a copy of your "Reef Notes" for November 1989, because he knew I was having a similar problem with my reef tank in keeping corals alive (and especially anemones). The coral seems to do all right for about six months and then dies off (tongue, hammerhead, *Goniopora*). During this time the polyps never seem to extend fully, and the anemones never open up as they appear to be dying as soon as they are placed in the reef tank. I then placed the anemones in my other tank (a plain old 55 gallon with one light strip and undergravel filter) and the anemones all came back to life and open up fully. The water quality in the reef is perfect, while the 55 has some nitrates (40ppm).

The main point of this letter is that I feel the lighting on the reef tank is the cause of my problems. The reef tank is a 125 gallon glass tank with two VHO 140 watt Actinic 03, and two HO 85 watt daylights. I recall in your article that you obtained the spectral information for the daylights and that they appear to have a high U.V. component. First, wouldn't the water absorb this radiation in the first couple of inches? And secondly, I was told that once a bulb ages for about two weeks, this U.V. component drops to nothing.

Also you stated in the article that you placed a U.V.-absorbing lens over the bulbs. I mentioned this to my favorite pet store and they looked in their supply books and even called their wholesalers, but they were unable to find a supplier for the lens. Could you please give this information to me, or do you think that there might be another cause for the problem? In addition, if these lenses were placed over the bulbs, don't you have to worry about the lens melting from the heat of the bulbs? And, finally, would you suggest that I replace the fluorescent bulbs with a combination of two or three 175 watt metal halides and two 40 watt Actinic 03 bulbs? If you have any additional suggestions I would appreciate them. Thank you for your time, and I look forward to your reply. Sincerely, Jim Rohrbacher, Nashua, New Hampshire

A. I'm glad that you asked if I thought "there might be another cause" other than the lights, because yes I do. I think the consistent difficulty you've been having with anemones and hard corals is due to the temperature in your reef tank being too warm. The high intensity of light over your reef tank versus your more simply outfitted 55 gallon set-up would result in a significant temperature difference between the tanks, and would explain the response of the anemones. Then, again, you might write me back to tell me that you have a chiller on the reef tank, but I doubt it.

The lighting you are using should give superb results. I have seen the same lighting combination used many times with great success. Still, if the heat generated by the bulbs is allowed to bring the temperature of the aquarium above 80° F, the results with many organisms will be sacrificed.*

The U.V. component of the daylights is significant, though as I have pointed out in a previous column, fine results can be achieved without the installation of a U.V. absorbing lens, and this is mostly a result of two reasons. First, many photosynthetic organisms can tolerate significant doses of U.V., though their tolerance often varies due to exposure. Second, these U.V. emissions are absorbed by the water, but this will depend on the clarity of the water and the intensity of the bulbs. No, the "first couple of inches" does not remove all U.V., and the

*Although natural reefs often reach 86° F or slightly higher, the temperature range in closed aquariums is less flexible because of the saturation of dissolved oxygen. In the natural environment oxygen is maintained near or above saturation in the water by photosynthesis and wave action. In aquaria at high temperature the oxygen level in the water is lower than in nature at the same temperature.

Plastic sleeves do melt on H.O. and V.H.O. tubes. Therefore I no longer recommend using sleeves. It has been my experience that oftentimes what I thought were problems with UV could be solved with trace element additions (so probably the problem was photosynthetically produced excess oxygen in the tissues). Relocating an affected specimen also is helpful. I find no need to use a lens with fluorescent lamps, other than to prevent salt from encrusting the bulbs.

*Exception: When a metal halide fixture is suspended over an open aquarium, less heat accumulates than when fluorescents are used in a closed canopy.

U.V. emissions do not drop off after two weeks — a salty rumor if ever I heard one. Nevertheless, it should be pointed out that all bulbs lose intensity, and may change in spectral output with use.

The lenses I referred to are called Arm-A-Lite sleeves, manufactured by Thermoplastic Processes. You can find them by calling a plastics distributor in your area — hey, it's true that the guys at your local pet shop can work wonders sometimes, but there are many useful products for reef aquaria that you have to hunt down in other industries, with patience and ingenuity. Regarding the melting of lenses, yes, this can be a problem. Two solutions exist. If you are using "tombstone-end" type fixtures for your fluorescents, instead of waterproof end caps, the sleeves can be centered over the bulb with a pair of black end pieces that can be found in most lighting stores. These "caps" are used for centering bulb-protecting or colored sleeves over fluorescent bulbs. I have not tried to use these caps on HO and VHO bulbs, and fear they might burn with these lights. It has been my experience that the sleeves do warp and stick to the bulbs at the hot ends. Therefore, the other solution is to cut the lens so that it does not cover the last five inches on each end of the bulb. Finally, you may have difficulty locating the proper length lenses — it is possible that not all lengths are available. Good luck!

Oh, yes, you had still one more question. Regarding the metal halides, you must first control the suspected temperature problem before considering them.* I promised last month that a series was in the works describing lighting experiments using metal halide sources. The first article is complete and should appear soon with some important discoveries and observations. If you have not done so already, please read Peter J. Mohan's "Ultraviolet Light in the Marine Reef Aquarium," which appeared in the January 1990 issue of this magazine. The article is excellent, well times, and contains a very thorough list of references.

Q. I have had a 30 gallon reef tank set up for about a year. It has a "hang-on" type wet/dry filter and is lit by four Actinic white bulbs. It is full of live rock with an interesting assortment of invertebrates and macroalgae. The problem has become the small anemones which have taken over the tank. They are dark to light brown in color and seem to reproduce at an alarming rate. They are attached securely to the live rock and I have not been able to keep them under control. I have tried various mechanical removal means, including scraping and cutting them in two with scissors, but they show a remarkable ability to regenerate. I wouldn't mind a few, but is there a way to control them?

In addition, I read your March column's answer to the bristle worm problem. I seem to have several of these, too, but they have shown no appetite for anything beyond fish food. Should they not be helping my anemone problem? David W. Nolen, Wexford, Pennsylvania

A. I know I covered this one last time, but I'll discuss the problem again because I got this letter, and because of a recent conversation with Bruce Carlson, Acting Director of the Waikiki Aquarium. Last time I mentioned Wilken's recommended use of *Chelmon rostratus*, the copperbanded butterfly.

Bruce suggests putting a racoon butterfly, *Chaetodon lunula*, to work. If the corals can be removed for a few days, or the aquarium is large enough, one or more of these can be employed for the purpose of extracting the plague of *Aiptasia* sp. anemones. Can a bristle worm plague control the other? Unfortunately no, it can't, in this case. Try capturing the worms at night with the fish food. When the lights are off they tend to come out in the open.*

*Please refer to other suggestions in this book about *Aiptasia* and about bristle worms.

Q. I have a piece of hammer coral that seems to be "sprouting" at the hard skeletal base. It looks like the larger polyps, and I'm sure the little "bud" wasn't there when I bought the piece. Will the corals need a calcium supplement, and how do I supply it? I rarely feed at all. Sincerely, Jerry Libra, Austintown, Ohio

A. I have seen examples and photographs, and heard reports of such "budding" in Hammer coral (*Euphyllia ancora*), Elegance coral (*Cataaphyllia jardinei*),

*There is a difference between use of liquid "foods" and trace elements. I'm afraid I was not very precise in my answer. Trace element additions are essential to the long term health of reef aquariums. Trace elements are added via supplements, make-up water, and even with the fish food. To clarify, I do recommend adding trace element supplements. Other liquid "foods" can be beneficial, but must be added conservatively, as they can pollute the tank and contribute to proliferation of undesirable algae species.

Goniopora sp., and Plate coral (*Fungia* sp, and *Heliofungia* sp.). Still, do not wish to belittle the importance of the event in your aquarium. Congratulations!

I'm glad that you asked about supplements because I have some useful information for you. Readers of this column should be keenly aware of my very conservative position regarding the addition of foods and nutrients to a closed system reef tank. The healthiest displays I have seen have been maintained with very few additions to the water* and, conversely, the poorest exhibits have typically been "fed" heavily with supplements of various sorts. It is reasonable to assume that in a closed system, the nutrient input resulting from food additions for the fish alone compromises sufficient nutrients for most invertebrates, and can easily result in eutrification of the system because of its closed nature. Nevertheless, experience dictates that, despite the natural production of food items on the rock, many fish still need to be fed to maintain their optimal health. And likewise, despite the unlimited supply of essentials such as nitrogen, phosphorus, and carbon compounds, many invertebrates still must have certain nutrients replenished.

In my experience, the bulk of this requirement for the invertebrates is met by simply keeping a regular routine of partial water changes, and I'm certain that excellent success can be had indefinitely, without any trace substance additions, provided regular water changes are performed. However, there is an alternative, and that, of course, is to add specific important elements or compounds which are depleted with time by the invertebrates. If one is utilizing a sophisticated filtration system capable of completely removing the compounds and substances which become detrimental as they accumulate, i.e., nitrate, phosphate, complex organics, detritus, then a carefully regulated regimen of trace additions could greatly prolong the use of a given volume of sea water. I am aware of the practice of maintaining reef aquaria without water changes, and have done so as well for extended periods. In my experience, the practice can be done successfully with many of the invertebrate and plant species commonly available, as well as fish, but despite the novelty of it, the method stagnates

*I have seen and maintained aquaria with very little water change, but with regular addition of trace elements and calcium hydroxide. When the supplements are added and protein skimming is used, the water remains excellent. Some salt needs to be added periodically to replenish what is lost via the protein skimmer or spray. I still recommend that novices change about 25% of the water per month. I recognize now that a well balanced aquarium with complete biological filtration (i.e.natural reduction of nitrate in the substrate), protein skimming, supplementation of trace elements and use of calcium hydroxide may not need water changes.

**kalkwasser alone will maintain or raise alkalinity when dosed properly.

***Oops! The water used to make kalkwasser should not be heated! Ca(OH)$_2$ is one of a few substances that become less soluble in water with increase in temperature.

progress that can be made in the successful culturing of those species which don't fare well in such aquaria. What I'm leading to is a compromise which offers the best results.*

Follow a regular routine of partial water changes that includes the removal of detritus, be conservative with food additions, but don't starve the fish and, perhaps, add specific trace substances. I say perhaps because I am currently experimenting with the addition of certain elements to determine any benefits or disadvantages, and I do not wish to make any premature evaluations, despite the fact that the formulations and dosages I am using have been developed and successfully applied by several reputable hobbyists and authors in Europe for many years.

To focus back on your intended question, the addition of calcium to the water as Ca(OH)$_2$, or "kalkwasser" is considered very beneficial by many aquarists. Its addition is supposed to enhance the growth of coralline algae, which has a reciprocal effect of inhibiting undesirable algae. It is also used to replenish the calcium removed from the water by stony corals. Natural seawater has a calcium concentration of 400 mg/liter. One can maintain this level through the addition of "kalkwasser," but one must also observe the subsequent effect on the carbonate hardness of the water, which will fall as one adds kalkwasser. Ideally the carbonate hardness is maintained at about 7 to 8 degrees by the occasional addition of commercially available buffers**, and monitored by using commercially available KH test kits. One may wish to contact Hach, Inc. to obtain a calcium test kit. Kalkwasser is prepared by dissolving calcium hydroxide in heated*** pure water until a saturated solution is reached. This will occur when no more of the calcium hydroxide will dissolve, leaving some powder on the bottom of the container. When the mixture has settled and cleared, one decants the clear solution, the kalkwasser, into another container, being careful not to stir up too much undissolved calcium hydroxide. This saturated solution may then be added to the make-up water used to replace evaporation, so that only a dilute solution is added to the aquarium on a regular basis in order to maintain the proper concentration of calcium in the water.

On a lighter subject ...

I was surprised by the rapid response I've been getting to my question about why there were so many more men keeping reef aquaria than women. Linda Mack of Vallejo, California, admits men "do come in handy when it comes to lifting those boxes of live rocks." Simon D. Ellis of Mahwah, New Jersey, offered several possibilities, though female readers are likely to disagree with some of his reasoning:

(1) Keeping an aquarium — particularly a marine reef aquarium — is a messy proposition at best. How many of us have rinsed out that prefilter sponge only to have our noses assailed by the most foul of odors. Or two arms deep into 18 inches of saltwater in an attempt to relocate a 20 pound piece of live rock — all the time with a wary eye on that rogue mantis shrimp that evades every attempt to be caught. Perhaps not an attractive hobby for most women.

(2) Oh, I forgot about the foul brew from the protein skimmer.

(3) It is inevitable, no matter how careful one tries to be, that one will get water on the rug!

(4) I wonder if the fact that many aquaria involve a level of gadgetry, or mechanical support, attracts men (remember the adage that "the difference between men and boys is the price of their toys"), but repels most women. Not that women couldn't be just as accomplished, just that they are not interested.

(Item number 4 intrigues me, and it applies as well to hot rod automobiles, stereo equipment, and luxury yachts. I had this in mind when I asked the question. Item number 3 doesn't seem to apply, and I wish you hadn't mentioned it because it's been a secret of mine for years.)

Marianne Windish, secretary in the Bucks County Aquarium Society of southeastern Pennsylvania, offers some additional insights that nicely complement Mr. Ellis' first two assumptions. She would "rather vacuum out a fish tank any day than scrub a pot or the toilet,"

and adds, "why aren't more females into reefs? They are
maintaining homes. While men have wives, girlfriends,
or mothers cooking, house cleaning, washing clothes,
tending the kids, entertaining, and shopping, the woman
who is doing all of those things probably also has a job
outside of the home, and usually her husband or
boyfriend is not minding the house so she can hang over
the fish tank. How many men say, 'You enjoy the fish
tank, honey, while I do the housework.' And the average
daughter of the woman who is not maintaining a reef
does not have a female hobbyist role model to emulate."

And for the winner of the "Now, isn't that special" award.

Dear Julian,
I am writing in response to your question in FAMA's
March issue of "Reef Notes" regarding a woman's position
in the reef hobby. My husband and I have a 75 gallon
tank he gave me as a Christmas present. After moving into
our new home, we found the perfect place for our piece
of the reef, in our den. Working side by side we built the
DLS holder and sump out of glass given to us by a friend,
measured and cut the eggcrate, and cut the drip plates,
and drilled the holes for them. Together with some help
from our seventeen year old son, we designed and imple-
mented everything we wanted for our system.
John, my husband, does most of the drawing and
designing for our system. He designed the PVC line for
the water flow through our system. I do most of the
work on keeping the water chemistry in balance. I also
do 95% of the reading, keeping abreast of what's new
and trying out the ideas on our tank. FAMA is one of my
main sources (I only wish it came twice a month!).
Martin Moe's *The Marine Aquarium Reference Systems
And Inverts*, and Thiel's *The Marine Fish And Invert Reef
Aquarium* are also kept in my library as valued
resources.

A woman's place in the hobby depends on the woman.
My opinion is that couples who build things together
and share common interests are more likely to stay
together than those couples who share no interests at all.

So you see, Julian, a woman's place in the hobby — at

least in our home — is with her arm elbow deep in the reef. Sincerely, Melanie W. McMillan

July 1990

Before getting into the questions this month I wanted to add a few important comments about the use of kalkwasser, which I discussed briefly last month. When I began adding kalkwasser to my aquarium and others that I am now maintaining, I noticed an initial and sudden decline in Kh. In my own aquarium the Kh fell from about 7.5 dKh to about 5 dKh in a little over a week. All of these aquaria are maintained with natural seawater. I also received feedback about similar experience in aquaria utilizing artificial seawater (Charles Delbeek, pers. comm.). Nevertheless, this Kh drop does not always occur, or if it does, it does so only temporarily (Charles Delbeek, pers. comm. and pers. obs.). Hence, the problem is not a chronic one as I may have indicated last month.*

*It depends on dosage. If too much is added to the tank, the pH rises too high temporarily, causing a loss of alkalinity via precipitation of calcium carbonate.

I anticipate questions regarding the dosage which I intentionally left vague. It seems there are some who add dilute solutions to the aquarium, while others add pure saturated calcium water. Some add it periodically while others use it exclusively for the make-up water. For this reason I chose to simply recommend the maintenance of natural seawater concentration of calcium, 400 mg/L. It is an interesting observation of those aquarists who add pure saturated calcium water to their aquariums as the exclusive make-up water, that the concentration of dissolved calcium in the aquarium's water never exceeds 400 mg/L.** I was initially astounded that one could add the stuff at a rate determined solely by evaporation. This made no sense unless the excess would simply fall out of solution, which appears to be what happens when kalkwasser made from calcium hydroxide is used, as it has very low solubility. If, however, one adds a calcium chloride solution to the aquarium, the concentration of dissolved calcium can be made to exceed 400 mg/L. I have seen no data nor heard of any results associated with calcium levels elevated above normal saturation.*** In future columns I will present some of my own findings along with the commentary of other aquarists.

**It certainly can exceed 400 ppm with kalkwasser addition. It depends on the dosage.

***In future columns I explain how calcium chloride also depletes alkalinity.

One other important note ... If one is storing saturated

calcium water, the container should be labeled to avoid accidental ingestion, and sealed to avoid exposure to air which can make the calcium begin to fall out of solution.

Q. I wanted to share with you the enclosed photograph of my elegant coral, *Catalaphyllia jardinei*. The photo shows little black dots that would start in the middle of the coral's body and work their way out to the tips of its tentacles. During the summer this seemed to happen every couple of weeks, usually a day or two after I had fed it. I seem to think that my elegant coral is trying to reproduce... Sincerely, Jeff Joos, Kettering, Ohio

A. Well Jeff, ya stumped me, sort of. I'd like to tell you exactly what the black dots are, but I'm afraid I've never seen them before. I don't think they are related to reproduction, but I won't rule that possibility out. I suspect that they are "bundles" of zooxanthellae, but why they are so bundled and why they travel up the tentacles is a mystery to me. I am presenting your photo (Photo #1) and description here in the hopes of gaining the attention of someone in the field of coral research who might either be intrigued by your observations or have some insight about the cause. Please keep watching your coral and taking notes. I am curious about the path these spots travel and how long they last. Also, I'm especially intrigued about the correlation with feeding. I would very much appreciate it if you would keep in touch about this matter.

Q. I have a question concerning lighting using quartz halogen on reef tanks. Where are they on the ultraviolet scale? Can they be used? Sincerely, James Davie, Vanetten, New York

A. A good question. How many of us reef keeping fools have been shopping the local hardware/home improvement store and come around the corner of an isle to be suddenly blinded by a most powerful light source that is typically on sale for under thirty dollars ... fixture with bulb included? We have all wondered if quartz light sources could be used, and some have even tried them. As with any high intensity light source, the problems of heat and ultraviolet must be overcome for successful application. The fixtures I have seen have all had a glass *halogen bulbs are very yellow and emit little or no UV. They emit a lot of heat!*

lens mounted below the bulb. This would filter out some U.V., but would still allow some through.* They tend to run quite hot, but the effect on the water temperature can be managed with fans, air conditioning, or chillers. Nevertheless, the amount of infra-red emitted might elevate the temperature of the coral animals themselves. This is a problem I discussed as a hypothetical cause for the observation of so-called "burning" of coral tissue made by some hobbyists using metal halide light sources, when U.V. burning can be ruled out because of the use of the proper lens.

Now, you might ask if I have tried quartz halogen fixtures. I haven't, so I can only comment on what I have seen and heard from reliable sources. I have seen the prolific growth of numerous species of macroalgae under quartz lighting, but the corals did not appear to be thriving. I have heard of similar experiences from other hobbyists, but now I wonder if perhaps the lights were not properly used, or if there were other factors in the lack of success.

Interestingly, in one successful application a hobbyist informed me that the corallimorpharian *Ricordea florida* had multiplied at a fantastic rate throughout his aquarium. While other corallimorphs typically multiply rapidly under most types of lighting, *Ricordea* tends to just live, or if it multiplies, it does so very slowly. Rapid proliferation is very unusual. So, you might experiment with these lights, if you can deal with the heat. Some organisms may do very well, while others may not. Let me know how it goes for you.

Q. I am writing in regard to an article in the April issue of FAMA in your Reef Notes section, specifically the column on *Aiptasia*. I have known them as brown tube anemones. You said to inject them with potassium chloride to eradicate them. Since I have always had these creatures occupying every part of my 55 gallon aquarium, I need to know what concentration level of potassium chloride to use. I also need to know whether this will affect in any way the water quality or any other aspect of my reef aquarium. Sincerely, Jim Rasmusson, La Crosse. Wisconsin

A. I goofed! The recommendation should have been to use potassium hydroxide at a 15% concentration. I don't think any harm would be done if KCL were used, but maybe it doesn't work as well as KOH. Judging by the picture your description creates, I 'd have to recommend that you consider the alternative of biological control that I mentioned. A copperband or raccoon butterflyfish sounds a lot easier than a thousand tiny injections. If you feel you must go the injection route, don't worry, the KOH won't affect your water quality when used in small quantities.*

*Please review all suggestions for *Aiptasia* in this book.

Q. I have just recently ventured into an interest in saltwater aquariums. I have just successfully operated two 30-gallon freshwater tanks for the past year and am now ready to take on more of a challenge. However, the cost of purchasing a reef tank, wet/dry filter, is costly. Also, the potential designs seem to be endless, along with the cost!

Having then recovered from the initial shock, I have decided to build my own system . I'd like to know if you can help me sift through the deluge of information available. I have listed some of the information I need:

(1) A "hardware store buildable" system capable of at least 200 gallons.

(2) Is it true that I should consider only 50% of the blueprint's design? Example: 200 gallon wet/dry is actually good for 100 gallon tank.

(3) Saltwater aquariums with only the bottom glass being used (no substrate). You did write briefly about this idea in the October '89 issue, can I have more information on this? Thank you.

(4) What is the least expensive way to quietly pump water back to the tank ? (powerheads vs. submerged vs. exterior pumps) .

(5) What ratio of gallons in aquarium to gallons pumped per hour, at what foot head ?

(6) I read all kinds of "sale promotionals" on biological filter media, from taking nylon sold in clothing stores for quilts, and house gutter screening, rolling lightly like a HO-HO then stacking, to the expensive but seemingly well liked and advertised Bio-Pak. May I have your opinion please? Sincerely, Phillip Des Rosiers, Lackawanna, NY

A. (1) I won't design it for you and rob you of the satisfaction, but you can build your own filter using 1/4 inch salvage glass, an old or new 20 gallon long or high, or 30 gallon long aquarium, and eggcrate pieces attached together with cable ties for the partitions. Take time considering all aspects of the design. If you are using an external pump, plan on having holes drilled at a glass shop, and be sure to buy bulkhead fittings before you drill to be sure you have the right size (the bit will fit over the end of the bulkhead).

(2) Nonsense. I will have more to say about this after I answer your other questions.

(3) I have written more than briefly on the topic of reef tanks using no bottom sand or gravel. Basically the reasoning is that it affords a cleaner system and makes it easier to manage the accumulation of detritus. In a healthy reef tank using live rock for the reef structure, the bottom is soon painted purple and pink by the encrusting coralline algae, and soft corals or zoanthids placed on the bottom rapidly attach and spread on the glass, a very nice effect in my opinion. Still, it is a matter of personal preference whether you want sand or not.*

*see appendix for advantages of bottom substrate.

(4) Least expensive? This should not be your primary goal. The difference in price for pumps is not so great in the long run that you should consider cost first. Quietness is a reasonable consideration. Submersible pumps (including powerheads) offer very quiet operation, but their output is limited. External pumps tend to be a bit noisier, but afford greater output. When choosing an external pump it is also important to consider heat transfer to the water. Some pumps are capable of elevating the temperature a few degrees. . . not a desirable feature at all. By all means consult with some hobbyists who have been using different pumps for years and ask them pertinent questions about

reliability, heat added to the water, and output. Also note that the diameter of plumbing used has a dramatic impact on the volume pumped to the aquarium.

(5) This question follows naturally. Typically, home reef aquaria subject the return pumps to between four and six feet of head. This depends on the dimensions of your aquarium and stand, so recommendations don't apply. The literature on reef aquaria recommends anywhere from two to six complete turnovers per hour through the filter. Many have arbitrarily chosen three turnovers per hour as ideal, and some hobbyists go so far as to suggest that exceeding the ideal they have set would be detrimental. I have indicated in this column that in an aquarium full of live rock such specific turnover recommendations are ridiculous, and if the return pump is the sole means of providing water motion, these recommendations really don't afford adequate flow for some organisms. Turning over the entire volume of the tank so many times per hour does not insure that the water really moves in the aquarium, as it should. In deciding on a return pump rate for the filter in a reef tank utilizing live rock as the reef structure, I recommend that you choose the maximum capacity your drainage and filter can handle safely ... that is if you even wish to have such a filter, a subject I'll discuss in just a moment.

(6) My opinion is simply this: With the exception of media that might leach substances into the aquarium or clog with detritus and bacterial slime, all other inert materials are just fine to use. You might consider commercially available media for their uniform, neat, or colorful appearance, which is an aesthetic decision, not a biological one, especially in a reef tank.

In a recent phone conversation with Charles Delbeek I learned that German aquarist Dietrich Stüber has long been running his aquarium with no wet/dry or external biological filter at all, only a protein skimmer. Charles subsequently sent me photos of Stüber's aquarium which is truly a spectacular garden. Large healthy branching colonies of the stony coral *Seriatopora* * have sprung up from the live rock. A colony of the staghorn coral, *Acropora* sp. has grown to fill a large section of his

*Actually it is
Pocillopora
damicornis.

aquarium, touched down and encrusted on adjacent live rock at the front of the aquarium, and sent up healthy new branches with normal morphology. All exposed surfaces are heavily coated by red, purple, and pink coralline algae. Still more recently (yes I pay a hefty phone bill), aquarist and author Alf Jacob Nilsen emphatically confirmed that he and many others share the same philosophy. (Alf Nilsen, pers. comm.). It seems many of these hobbyists have essentially concluded that they didn't have true reef tanks until they removed their wet/dry filters, an admission which might astound American hobbyists, but which comes as no surprise to me. Most continue to use large protein skimmers, typically without ozone, and they use activated carbon to clarify the water. The use of other types of equipment such as redox meters, CO_2 injection, and dosing pumps varies as a matter of personal preference.

Emperor's clothing?...

"No filter?" you might ask. Yes, no external biological filter, but the aquaria are established with live rock exclusively, and it accomplishes the biological filtration. Obviously, in a heavily populated fish aquarium without live rock or other potential internal "media" this would not work. I have been running my own reef aquarium without an external biological filter for over a year now. It is densely populated with both fish and invertebrates and I don't feel that my aquarium has any less capacity for its lack of filtration. Still most hobbyists I have spoken to do not feel as confident as I do that in an established reef tank with live rock, the filter media can be completely removed at once with no harm done. Nevertheless, these same hobbyists are quick to admit that they confidently maintained heavy populations of fish for years in aquaria where the biological filtration was accomplished merely by flowing water over a bed of gravel in which only the surface inch was really performing the nitrification. In a reef tank you not only have potentially more aerobic surface area for the bacteria, you also have anemones, corals, and plants which don't pollute the water with nitrogenous waste, and actually filter it out of the water. Also, each rock contains the perfect proximity of aerobic and anaerobic zones which allows for denitrification to proceed naturally as it does on the reef, and live rocks already contain the right microorganisms.

I wish an unbiased, meticulous study could be made that compared (a) the populations of bacteria present in a wet/dry filter seeded and established inorganically, (which would contain a large proportion of the nitrifying bacteria we accept as being essential permanent components in the filter), with (b) bacteria populations in a filter likewise established but run for a period of months or years on a reef tank with live rock and fish. Knowledge of the difference would be valuable. Other useful comparisons could show the change in bacteria population over time on fish-only systems, and the ability to "recover" capacity in systems experiencing long periods without ammonia input. As always, one has to understand my position that you can have a satisfying and successful reef aquarium using many very different techniques and philosophies. It is hard to argue that someone is wrong if he is really successful using techniques that I suggest are not desirable, or if he is not following what I say is preferable but is still having great success. Therefore, in this month's column I am not attempting to undermine the aquarium industry which has seen a tremendous period of growth as a result of the acceptance of wet/dry filtration and the ability to maintain living reef displays. I am only pointing out that such aquaria can be well maintained independent of the wet/dry filter, and that there are reputable, experienced aquarists who have determined that their own systems at least perform better minus the external biological filter.

Few aquarists really took Lee Chin Eng seriously years ago when his natural method was considered possible but risky and perhaps too delicately balanced. Now it seems that many are rediscovering the method with a few added pieces of technology for even better results.

One more subject to keep your level of interest up. While I have always encouraged maintenance measures that tend to promote the most nutrient poor environment in our closed system reefs, and I will continue to do so as a closed system must be carefully regulated, I wanted to describe to you the type of environment most of the species available to aquarists come from. For a combination of biological, and no doubt economic reasons, the majority of the invertebrates we keep are collected on near-shore reefs where the water is not as nutrient poor as the offshore reefs, is often quite turbid because of run-off of mud and clay from the land, and the temperature is less stable than at offshore reefs. In Australia I found most of the species of hard and soft corals that we see in aquaria occurring on reefs near shore or around islands within a few miles of the continent. Forty miles out on the clear, nutrient poor Great Barrier Reef I did not see the Pipe organ, Bubble, *Euphyllia, Turbinaria,* and Elegance corals that I had seen on the muddy, turbid inshore reefs. Interestingly, *Goniopora* was common to both environments, though I noticed more species on the inshore reefs. These inshore reefs were quite prolific, with many species of hard and soft coral, and dense growth of marine plants covering and shading healthy coralline algae, and corals, though the density of the plants varies with the seasons. On the offshore Great Barrier Reef, exposed surfaces were generally coated by pink coralline algae, and dense plant growth was nonexistent except for the occasional small patch of "Turtleweed," *Chlorodesmis* sp. On the top of the reef, by the way, I found and photographed a nice healthy patch of "red slime" algae, cyanobacteria. I thought it might make some of you feel better to know that.

The ever-popular elegance coral, *Catalaphyllia jardinei* (which has been described as fussy about water purity), I found growing in the mud! One large healthy head which I extracted by painstakingly rocking it back and forth twenty feet down while holding my breath had a very nice sulfur smell eminating from its thoroughly black, anaerobic base. Of course I carefully replaced the coral where I had found it. *Catalaphyllia's* special ability to thrive in this environment is owing to its capacity to rid itself of a sediment coating, the conical shape of its skeleton, and its ability to inflate its tissues with water in such a way as to lift itself up and prevent burial. (P. Laboute, 1988). Still many hobbyists successfully grow this coral for years, with the skeleton increasing in size by inches (and the tissue sometimes by feet, nearly), when the specimen is propped up on live rock.

That's all folks.

References Laboute, P. 1988. The presence of scleractinian corals and their means of adapting to a muddy environment: the "Gail Bank." Proceedings of the 6th International Coral Reef Symposium, Australia, 1988, 3:107-111.

August 1990

Hello everyone, I'd like to take a moment to remind you all of my eternal request for photographs of your reef tanks. As I explained a few months ago, I'd like to feature a few of them to offer everyone a view of just how different such aquaria may appear when maintained under different circumstances. I have been disappointed in your response since I have received photographs from only one hobbyist so far. Please, let's see a shot of your pride and joy.

Many thanks to everyone who responded to my question about women's vs. men's involvement in the reef keeping hobby. I'm sorry I'm not going to publish any more of the letters, as the June issue contained enough, but I really enjoyed the enthusiastic response and amusing comments.

Can you imagine a fish that eats bristle worms? Well it so happens there are many fish that do, and gladly swim around with a face full of white bristles for the reward of the tasty pink morsel underneath. The Red Sea basslets, *Pseudochromis springeri*, and *P. dutuoiti* * have been observed with many a bristly grin (Charles Delbeek, pers. comm.), as have many wrasse species. A number of hobbyists have informed me that the banded coral shrimp, *Stenopus hispidus* relishes bristle worms as well.

*Actually the fish most commonly imported is *P. aldabraensis*, although the common name in the trade for this fish is still "*dutuoiti*."

While we're on the subject of who-eats-who, I'd like to comment on one of my favorite additions to reef tanks — the brittle stars — and an exception which some hobbyists, myself included, have noted. Serpent stars are generally very desirable in the reef tank, and I recommend that every tank contain several of them as they are excellent scavengers, always catching those bits of food that the fishes miss, which get carried by the current to points inaccessible. There are many fabulously colored and patterned ones as well, including brilliant, artificial-looking but quite natural day-glow orange, deep green with white bands and polka-dots, maroon, brick red with white bands, and yellow. These are all smooth armed brittle stars, often called serpent stars for the snake-like appearance of the arms. Aside from their neat appearance and biological function in the ecology of a closed system reef, they also are fascinating to watch as they scurry with great speed and precision toward a piece of food, with a sense of smell so good it rivals vision, and delicately coil an arm around the food as they swiftly pass it up into the mouth under their central disc. Recent experience has led me to make an exception concerning the behavior of one spectacular looking type of brittle star; the giant spiny variety which may be black, brown, or reddish with black spines. The Atlantic species is *Ophiocoma echinata*, and it can grow to over a foot across. As far as I know they occur in all tropical reef areas, but the species may be different in the various locales. Though they are frighteningly charming little beasts, they have undesirably liberal taste buds, and may suddenly feast on soft-coral polyps (Mike Paletta, pers. comm.), or *Tridacna* spp. clams (pers. obs.). Mike described to me recently how one very large specimen in his reef tank very methodically would grab hold of a polyp of *Anthelia* with one arm, and delicately remove one tentacle at a time with another, as if playing she-loves-me-not with a daisy. It had a habit of doing this only at night so it took Mike a while to figure out who was chewing up the *Anthelia*. He placed the colony up near the top of the tank, beyond the normal range of the starfish, and it recovered. I'm sure that starfish is outta' there as soon as it can be caught. I have seen the spiny black brittle star reach into the incurrent siphon of healthy *Tridacna* spp. clams, and I have seen them reach up through the opening around the foot and byssus.

Q. I set up a mini-reef eight months ago in a 55 gallon acrylic tank. I am using two Actinic and two daylight bulbs to illuminate the tank about twelve hours each day. I am also using a wet/dry filter, Chemi-Pure™, and a small protein skimmer. The corals and fish appear fine.

Unfortunately, since the initial set-up I've had a problem with hard brown micro-algae. From what I've read this is fairly typical of new tanks. The algae growth has slowed down considerably over time, and *Turbo* Grazers keep the rocks looking presentable, but the growth on the front and sides of the tank is still unsightly. This algae is very hard to remove and cleaner magnets glide right over the stuff. I find that only hand scraping with an algae pad and considerable pressure will remove it. This disrupts the animals in the tank, has caused some scratches on the acrylic, and given me some painful stings/bites from coral and shrimp. Do you have any suggestions on how I can remove this algae less painfully? Is algae easier to remove from glass than acrylic? (I'll get another tank if necessary — the hand-scraping is that tiresome and time-consuming.) Thanks for any help you can give me. Sincerely, Linda Mack, Vallejo, California

A. I would not say that such hard brown algae is typical of new tanks, but it is not rare either. The tough-to-remove stuff is typical of older tanks, and includes a number of species. Interestingly, the hard brown spattering dots are more common in acrylic aquaria, whereas hard green dots are more common in glass aquaria. At least this has been so in my experience. I believe the brown alga on the front and sides of your aquarium is a type of diatom. Some other types of hard-to-remove encrusting algae you might see in a reef tank include: crustose corallines which form purple, pink, and maroon colored spots; the encrusting brown alga, *Ralfsia,* which forms large brown circular spots, and the newly settled growths of the red alga *Botryocladia,* which might be mistaken for coralline algae.

To answer your questions, yes, algae is easier to remove from glass than acrylic. A wide razor blade (detachable, replaced after each cleaning) affixed on a long stick easily removes the most stubborn algae growths from glass. It can scratch the glass if one is not careful, so be careful ... hold it flat against the glass, replace it if it gets a notch in the edge or if it is corroded. Is there a similar solution for acrylic aquaria? Well, sort of, but it will take a bit of experimenting on your part. The edge of a common credit card is almost as effective on acrylic as a blade is on glass. However, there is a tendency for the straight edge to wear down quickly, which makes it leave extremely undesirable streaks on the acrylic. Some credit cards will scratch some acrylic, and some combinations are less likely to do so ... I can be no more specific than that. Some "algae pads" are more effective than others, but all require serious elbow grease in order to remove tough spots. There are pads sold exclusively for acrylic tanks at your local pet store, and there are similar devices, often with nifty "ergonomic" handles attached, sold at your local supermarket. Many of these work really well but, beware that some supermarket pads can even scratch glass ... try it out on something other than your tank first. One of the advantages of a plastic straight edge or credit card over any pad is that the former does not pick up grains of sand which scratch the acrylic. Cleaning algae toward the base of the tank with a pad, one inevitably picks up particles which will trace neat parallel lines in your viewing window for everyone to see.

Q. I've been experimenting with a dissolved oxygen reactor in a 38 gallon reef tank and would like your help before I feel comfortable to continue.

The tank inhabitants are doing fine except for the hard corals. A *Goniopora* has retracted tentacles and a "finger" coral is receding from its skeleton. Soft corals like Star Polyp are doing extremely well and are spreading to adjoining rocks. One anemone has grown by 25% in a six month period.

I've been following your suggestions on tank maintenance to keep unwanted algae growth from occurring by minimizing food inputs, using RO water and maximizing outputs via 20% weekly water changes, tank substrate cleaning and daily prefilter cleaning. Even though this maintenance routine is carried out religiously, the tank still generates what I feel is a significant amount of green algae on the glass. The glass must be cleaned every two to three days and the algae is very difficult to remove unless a scraper is used.

Based on your comments from past issues of FAMA, it would appear I have high nutrient levels. Since I'm minimizing the external sources of nutrient inputs by using RO water and minimum food inputs (once a week for the fish only), the excess nutrients must be generated from within the tank. Given enough time and water changes, the levels may eventually subside. To speed the nutrient reduction along, I thought about using ozone. With the initial cost of the equipment and potential safety concerns, I've decided against it for now. Instead I built an oxygen reactor. A chemical engineer at work indicated that increasing the dissolved oxygen level is another way to improve conditions since excess oxygen will act as an oxidizing agent like ozone, but it will not be as aggressive.

Before starting the reactor, the baseline dissolved oxygen level in the tank was 5.9 ppm measured with a Lamotte test kit. After the reactor was hooked up and running at +2psi, dissolved oxygen levels were monitored for the next three days, measurements were taken at 24 hour intervals with the following results:

> 1st day 6.4ppm
> 2nd day 7.2ppm
> 3rd day 7.8ppm

As it was a homemade reactor, I was not expecting the levels to increase as they did in such a short period of time. On the third day, I was concerned with the continued rate of increase and disconnected the unit. Is there a possibility of overdosing with dissolved oxygen? This would be an OD on DO! (Sorry, I couldn't resist.) Seriously, is there a potential for harmful effects on tank inhabitants? What do you recommend as the maximum DO level that should be maintained?

Due to space limitations I connected the water output of the reactor to the inlet of the protein skimmer. I wanted to keep the reactor independent of the main aquarium pump. The reactor and skimmer are situated in the sump of the trickle filter and driven by a separate water pump. With this arrangement the protein skimmer stopped functioning. A 1/2 inch foam heat formed on the top of the skimmer with no signs of producing the usual levels of goop during the three days of testing. After disconnecting the reactor, the skimmer returned to its normal production levels. What happened? Does the level of dissolved oxygen have an impact on surface tension? Or was the reactor actually oxidizing the proteins, thus preventing the formation of the usual levels of foam? I would greatly appreciate any comments you have on these questions. Sincerely, Gary Nickerson, Wilbraham, Massachusetts

A. There are a number of details of interest in this letter. Regarding the stony corals receding from the skeleton or not doing well, I can only offer limited advice based on the limited information you gave. First, *Goniopora* is difficult to maintain for now until we figure out why, so don't feel bad if yours is not looking up to snuff. As I have indicated in this column, *Goniopora* typically shows off beautifully for several months, often up to a year, but eventually declines in most closed system aquaria. I do not know what species you mean by "finger" coral, but recession from the skeleton, as I have explained before in this column, is caused when something is preventing the coral from laying down new calcium, if it's not caused by some sort of insult or injury to the tissue. Numerous factors affect calcium deposition. The most common factors you should be concerned about, in order of importance, are light intensity, calcium availability in the water, and phosphate inhibition. The concentrations of other major and minor elements in the seawater also play a role, but these factors are generally less frequently the cause of this problem in most home aquaria, and considering your admirable 20% weekly water changes, they are not a factor in your aquarium.

Regarding the rapid growth of green algae on the glass, this is probably not a result of excessive nutrients. It probably is a result of the aquarium receiving some sunlight every day from a nearby window. The crusty algae which grow on the glass are rather efficient at utilizing any available nutrients, and will grow in proportion to the amount of light they receive. It is impossible to completely limit their nutrient supply in a closed system tank, and the longer their photoperiod, or the more intense the light during that period, the quicker they will grow. Don't get me wrong, I encourage the use of any available sunlight in reef aquaria, and consider it an important aid, as long as it doesn't elevate the temperature. Perhaps you have a long photoperiod on the tank. Try to light the aquarium for no longer than twelve hours, if you are not doing so already.

Live rocks and other substrates may store significant quantities of nutrients, so your idea about nutrients being generated within the tank is not so much wrong as it is probably not to blame for the green algae on the glass. I do not know whether you have any of the herbivorous snails in your aquarium, but let me recommend them to you as they may help your situation both directly and indirectly. If you have enough of them, they can significantly curb the growth of algae on the glass, thus directly assisting the maintenance. Their indirect affect is less obvious. As they polish off algal growth with one end, the other continually emits tightly packaged lightweight fecal pellets which drift around in the water column until they are either trapped by the prefilter, captured and consumed by a coral, or trapped behind the rocks in that detritus heap that you are supposed to vacuum once in a while. The net result is that they help export nutrients pulled from the water by the algae. You clean the prefilter and siphon the bottom, or the coral and other filter feeders metabolize the nutritious morsels. In the meantime, you will be honing your technique with the blade.

An oxygen reactor, for those of you who are not familiar with such devices, is a vessel into which both air and water are injected, the water's progress being slowed by some sort of inert media stuffing the vessel, so that the water has extended and extensive contact with the pressurized air, achieving supersaturation with oxygen. Such devices are also used at times with ozone for the purpose of quickly attaining and maintaining elevated redox potential values, but should not be operated with pure oxygen. (See Burleson, Reef Tips FAMA Vol. 12 #4, April 1989, for a thorough description.).

Your engineer friend was correct about elevating dissolved oxygen levels to improve water quality. Something I'm not sure that you are aware of, however, is that dissolved oxygen levels vary as a function of photosynthesis and respiration on an hourly basis in a pretty regular daily cycle when the lighting regime is regulated by a timer. It is good that you took the measurements at 24 hour intervals, as we can at least say that the reactor was elevating the dissolved oxygen levels. Oxygen saturation varies as a function of temperature, salinity, and atmospheric pressure (Moe, 1989), and these factors affect both the levels you will observe and the levels at which oxygen becomes toxic in your aquarium. On the subject of toxicity, I do not believe that you could elevate the dissolved oxygen to toxic levels using just air in the oxygen reactor at +2psi pressure. With pure oxygen as the gas injected under pressure, however, you could poison the aquarium (Burleson, 1989). I do not know at precisely what level of supersaturation of oxygen that the oxygen becomes toxic to invertebrates but, as I said, you needn't worry if you are using just air or even an air/ozone mixture.

The cessation of froth collection by your protein skimmer was a result of the reactor actually oxidizing the proteins, as you noted, but do not assume that this means the reactor's efficacy had purified the entire aquarium. Whereas true redox values approaching 500 millivolts in an aquarium, achieved through the application of ozone, will prevent protein skimming, the reason your skimmer wasn't working was due to its proximity to the reactor ... it was taking water directly from the reactor, as you noted, so it couldn't skim. It would be a better arrangement to separate these two devices.

Keep up the good work, Gary, and pay attention to the inverts' appearance as your guide when experimenting with "new frontiers" such as supersaturating dissolved oxygen.

Q. Do you have any suggestions for attaching animals such as corals or small rocks with anemones or zoanthids on them to the reef structure? I have tried silicone, a product called Adapt 4.5, monofilament fishing line, and even rubber bands, none of which has been really satisfactory. Best Regards, David Millon, Miami, Florida

A. Yeah, Dave, that's a good question. There are fewer things more frustrating in the reef-keeping hobby than coming home to find that same suicidal piece of coral lying "face" down on top of another coral or anemone in a game of "I'll burn you, you'll burn me." And it's true it doesn't take much coaxing by those terrific algae eating snails to knock half the reef down. That's why there's a new marine cement which bonds quickly to any surface underwater, is non-toxic, and remains flexible so that it doesn't shear apart when bumped. Trouble is, this cement exists only in our imagination, but maybe that will change.* For now we have a few less-than-perfect but certainly workable techniques. The Adapt 4.5 is non-toxic and remains flexible, but doesn't bond to the sub-strates. It is most useful as an aid to locking a specimen in place, providing a tight, flexible buffer or shim when a specimen can be inserted into a hole or crevice, but it won't stick one flat surface to another. Monofilament line is most useful for attaching soft corals to rocks. Don't be afraid to thread the line onto a long needle and pierce the base of a leather coral (*Sarcophyton*) or a *Dendronephthya* to tie it to a rock. These corals need only to be held in place for a week or so in order to give them opportunity to attach themselves. The monofila-ment serves this purpose well. Monofilament can also be used to tie rocks together, or occasionally to tie a stony coral to a more easily placed rock. Cable ties also come in handy for the same applications as monofilament. Rubber bands are similarly useful, and may be used for shimming as well. Even toothpicks can be jammed into the base of a stony coral or into a *Sarcophyton* to assist placement, and likewise plastic rods can be used for pegging the corals into the reef structure. I have seen good results obtained when small rocks were drilled with a 1/2 inch bit, more or less, for the creation of an easy-to-place base for soft corals such as Gorgonians. Finally, there's a technique which I have been using for years that you can use too, Dave, since you live in south Florida. I often use sponges as an aid to coral placement, but only certain sponge species work well for this pur-pose. The best ones are *Amphimedon* (*Haliclona*) *viridis,* a green finger sponge from the Atlantic and Caribbean, and *Chondrilla nucula*, a circumtropical rub-bery sponge which I have referred to before in this col-umn, using its common name, "chicken liver sponge." An undamaged small piece of either of these sponges

*At last, there really is such a thing. Several forms of underwater repair epoxy cement can be used safely and effectively in aquaria to adhere specimens to the rocks or to glass. Please see the aquas-caping section of *The Reef Aquarium, Vol. 1* by Delbeek and Sprung, for further information.

will attach a piece of coral to a rock within two days if carefully placed next to both without crushing the sponge. Needless to say, there is an art to this, and it takes some experience to become a good sponge sticker! While healthy chicken liver sponge is occasionally available to hobbyists with live rock, the only other species commonly available which is useful for this purpose is the lovely blue *Haliclona* species from Indonesia.

Q. I wrote once previously about an article of yours on metal halide lighting. My letter was in a somewhat negative tone, but this time I feel somewhat obliged to you, as I have tried an improvement on one of my tanks which was inspired by another of your articles, and which has worked extremely well. Beyond all expectations, in fact. So I thought I'd tell you about it.

The tank in question was a 50 gallon "Dutch" mini-reef, about eighteen months old. At the time, it wasn't in very good shape, and I wasn't to sure what to do about it. The homemade filter was beginning to hemorrhage internally (a lot of water was dripping around the trays instead of through them) and I was beginning to suspect the coral media was losing its effectiveness anyway. It wouldn't support more than two or three smallish fish, and it had a good, healthy growth of red cyanobacteria, and wouldn't support any plants at all (though the invertebrates were still very healthy. Don't ask me why. Good lighting I guess). Various convoluted plans came to mind involving the cycling of a parallel filter which would then be connected to the tank, etc. etc.

Then I read your article in which you mentioned bypassing the filter in one of your tanks altogether, and not noticing much difference. The rocks were doing the filtering. I suspected that I had unwittingly invoked the same situation in my troubled child so I bypassed its filter (the dry section, at least). Held my breath for two weeks: nothing happened. The tank looked exactly the same. (I videotape my tanks periodically in order to evaluate their progress.)

So this gave me the opportunity to remove those trays, and fill the thing with one of the plastic media, which I did, then reconnected the filter normally. This was possibly a somewhat heroic move on my part, but I seem to have been blessed with a hefty dose of dumb luck, if nothing else. There was no dry section anyway, so I figured, how could it hurt?

It's only been a couple of weeks, but the invertebrates are perkier, and the cyanobacteria is all but gone! What fish were there are still okay. I think that maybe the thing is gradually cycling itself, though I'm not seeing any measurable ammonia. Should I add biozyme or something? Since it will never be cycled in the traditional sense, I'm not too sure what the future holds for this tank, but the present is a definite improvement. Thanks! I guess the new media is, at the very least, providing a lot of aeration.

A: You're welcome. I will have more to say about this in the near future. Send pictures.

References Moe, M.A. Jr., 1989. *The Marine Aquarium Reference — Systems and Invertebrates.* Green Turtle Publications. Plantation, Fl. 512 pp.

Burleson, J. 1989. Reef Tips, FAMA: Vol. 12, No. 4, pp:120-121.

October 1990

Note: The photos could not be reproduced clearly in black and white. You will have to refer to the original article to see them.

I am including a couple of photographs this month of a 100 gallon reef tank which I maintain on Miami beach because of the unusual relationship that has developed between a siamese cat, "Platinum," and a spanish hogfish named Haydee (pronounced"Haiti.") Look, I swear this cat and this fish are buddies!

I am also including a photo of an elegance coral and a colony of *Cladiella* sp. soft coral, commonly called "colt coral," which I photographed in one of four reef tanks I helped set up for Exotic Aquaria, Inc. of North Miami at the 1990 Miami Beach Home Show. The colt coral and elegance coral began showing signs of what I believe is U.V. burning under fluorescent lighting two days into the show. The lighting included V.H.O. daylight bulbs which emit significant amounts of U.V. light. Notice that the polyps most exposed to the light remain closed, and the affected area has a greyish color, while those which are shaded, or which are below a critical depth, remain fully open. I have maintained *Cladiella* sp. under VHO daylights, close to the surface, without these symptoms developing, so it is somewhat of a mystery to me why this specimen was so distinctively affected. My observation of the species in the field may hold a clue ... *Cladiella* was most often growing on the sides of coral "bommies" in Australia, often between bommies, but seldom on top where they would be directly exposed. I did find many growing on the bottom as well, but usually in such a way that they would get direct illumination for only part of the day. I found many under overhangs. In contrast, the similar looking *Sinularia* species were common on the tops of coral bommies or on shallow bottoms where exposure to the sun was maximum.

The first two days of the show both the *Cladiella* and the large elegance coral were beautifully expanded. On the third day, however, both specimens showed similar symptoms. In the case of the elegance coral, those tentacles most exposed to the light down to a critical depth were contracted in appearance, and had an off-greyish color. Below this critical depth the tentacles were normal. It is hard to blame water conditions for these sudden changes considering the fact that the symptoms were only on portions of these corals which were most exposed to the light, and the fact that other specimens of the same species in the same tank, but lower down, were not affected. The aquarium had a chiller on it and was maintained at 74° F. I am telling you about this incident and showing you photographs because such symptoms have never been photographically demonstrated in an aquarium journal, only described. It is not my intention to whip up hysteria about the horrors of a particular bulb. VHO daylights are fine bulbs, and I use them extensively with excellent success. Still, the occasional incidence of UV "burning" is something that needs to be addressed. For you who are avid readers of this magazine, pardon me for being redundant, but for those who are not, please read Pete Mohan's article on UV light. (FAMA January, 1990.) In Reef Notes, I described a similar problem which occurred in my own aquarium, affecting a photosynthetic gorgonian., *Pseudoplexaura* sp.

(FAMA November, 1989). As I described, when I filtered out the UV spectrum with acrylic lenses, the affected portions of my gorgonian opened within two days. It concerns me that hobbyists observing these symptoms in their own aquaria might simply assume that they were over-illuminating the tank. I have heard many hobbyists claim just that for whatever reason. While an acrylic lens would solve the situation, many hobbyists unknowingly just avoid beefing up the intensity of light over the aquarium, and miss the substantial benefit this intensity has on the health of the corals.*

*It is possible that UV had something to do with the observed symptoms, either directly or indirectly, but I suspect that photosynthetically produced excess oxygen (superoxygen) was at least partly the cause. I have since learned that trace element additions are helpful in curing the symptoms.

I was amused by another incident at this same home show. While I was proudly explaining to an enthusiastic couple the life histories of some of the reef organisms in the aquaria, a guy walked up to the booth with a particular smirk which I recognized very well. He need not have said it for I knew what he was thinking. Saltwater? Impossible to keep, he was sure, and he had a story to back up his assertion. He had a saltwater tank some years back and everything died. It was a wipeout. Nobody could tell him what went wrong ... "the water checked out perfect."

No sooner had he rattled out his story and frustration than he was off floating down the aisle shaking his head and muttering something no doubt with a blameless conviction. I was wondering if I should have felt regret for not attempting to explain that there was an awful lot more to a successful tank than correct water chemistry, that life is not a perfect model of black and white rules governed exclusively by a few simple parameters with no further ramification. I wondered if the pet dealer had misled him. Come to think of it, my concerns about this guy's role in our hobby were beginning to sound religious. For the moment, I wished I had taken the time to set this guy straight, but considering his attitude, I'm glad he no longer has an interest in the hobby.

Still More On *Aiptasia*...

Q. In your April 1990 column you had a question regarding how to get rid of *Aiptasia* in an aquarium, and you mentioned that certain species of butterflyfish will eat

Aiptasia. Well, I'd like to report that the raccoon butterfly-fish, *Chaetodon lunula*, eats *Aiptasia* and therefore can be very effective in controlling those pesky anemones.

I first noticed this feeding behavior in our Edge Of The Reef exhibit about a year ago. I had put a rock covered with algae (and a few *Aiptasia*) into the tank to feed the herbivores, and noticed that the raccoon butterflyfish seemed to be picking off the little brown anemones. So I put in another rock, and sure enough, he/she went right for the *Aiptasia*.

With that in mind, I tried a little experiment in a reef tank that I had set up, which, within a period of about 3 weeks, had become overgrown with *Aiptasia*. I've enclosed a couple of pictures to show the results. Photo 4 is a shot of a rock with definite anemone infestation. Photo 5 was taken just 6 days later, after adding a small (about 4-5") raccoon butterflyfish. Keep in mind that my whole tank looked like the first photo, and after 6-7 days there were practically no anemones to be found. However, this may not be a cure for everyone's problems. Many butterflyfish will eat corals, and *Chaetodon lunula* is no exception. Putting a raccoon butterfly in a tank with live corals may be a little risky. When I first set up my tank, I had live rocks but no live corals in it. After ridding the tank of the *Aiptasia*, I then removed the raccoon butterflyfish and put in the corals (of course, it wasn't that simple — I had to remove most of the rocks first in order to get the fish out!), so far the tank is doing fine. There are a few *Aiptasia* growing but they don't seem to be spreading.

There may be other species of butterflyfishes that will eat anemones. Hobson (1974) studied the diets of various Hawaiian reef fishes and found that both the raccoon butterflyfish and the threadfin butterflyfish (*Chaetodon auriga*) fed on anemones. I hope this will help other aquarists, and would be interested to hear about other people's experiences with butterflyfishes in their reef tanks. Sincerely, Marjorie L. Awai Waikiki Aquarium 2777 Kalakaua Ave., Honolulu, Hawaii 96815

A. Thanks Marj!

Q. I enjoyed your column last month describing some of the small creatures of the mini-reef, but I have a few you didn't mention. I have a 45 gallon mini-reef tank which has been set up for approximately two years. The two creatures I'm interested in are:

(1) A small 1/2" to 1-1/2" long yellow worm. They usually stay hidden in the coral with their many tentacles exposed out of the coral. Occasionally I find them wandering on the glass, moving at a rate of about 2 feet per minute. Any idea what they are?

(2) Similar worms to the above, except they are a whitish, clear color, larger, 1-1/2" to 2" long with tentacles up to six inches long. They are never seen out of their hiding spots.

You also mentioned last month about *Aiptasia* anemones. Are these the whitish-clear to yellow colored, long-tentacled anemones you see in most mini-reef tanks? I have about six in my tank. They do reproduce, but few mature, probably because of being eaten. Some call these anemones a pest, but I like them. How do I increase their reproduction? (I know this sounds crazy, i.e., conditions, etc.) Thanks, Mike Jagadich, Bloomington, Illinois

A. I'll bet there's even someone out there who likes salt creep too! Well, you asked, so I guess I should tell you how to farm the little beasts in your aquarium, but don't go calling me if the neighbors start complaining when things get out of hand. Like most of the corals, you keep, Mike, *Aiptasia* harbor zooxanthellae, which means they obtain significant nourishment from photosynthesis. So one thing you could do to help them grow and reproduce faster is to provide more light. But that, alone, is only part of what it takes to make them really multiply. Extra nitrogen, particularly from high protein food and/or nitrate, also enhances their reproduction. Live brine shrimp poured into the aquarium will keep them well fed. Still more, the careless application of a blade, if you feel like mutilating your anemones today, will result in the production of more anemones. They naturally reproduce by a process called pedal laceration, in which they periodically pinch off portions of their base, the pedal disc, resulting in the formation of little brown lumps which miraculously become new *Aiptasia*s in a day or two. Their hardy nature makes them an ideal laboratory animal, which means that scientists have subjected them to an array of experiments in order to write something about them, so if you go to your nearest university library and look up anemones, zooxanthellae, and Cnidaria, and see the reference material in the back of the texts you find, or check these subject headings in periodical index-es, you are bound to find more info on them.

I have so talked about the worms you describe. They are terrebellid worms. Two feet per minute? No way! You must have meant two feet per hour unless your tank houses some sort of olympic spaghetti worm! The larger of the two you describe is an *Amphitrite* species, and these can get even larger, with tentacles reaching several feet in length.

Helpful Hints For The Month... The beautiful "Hammer coral," *Euphyllia ancora*, often suffers the attack of pro-tozoans as a result of shipping damage or simply for no obvious reason at all, but there is a very effective remedy that can be employed in order to save the specimen. I described the method briefly in "Reef Notes" when I mentioned the dreaded attack of the protozoan, *Helicostoma* sp. As was demonstrated for me by Bruce Carlson, Director of the Waikiki Aquarium, a freshwater dip is most effective. My initial impression was that the affected area only should be dipped, and that this would kill off the protozoan and a little healthy tissue near the affected area, but save the rest of the coral. I was some-what amazed when Bruce showed me that the entire coral colony could be left in freshwater for extended periods* with no harm done whatsoever, except to the protozoan. Now having performed this procedure on several affected colonies, I am confident in its safety. I have completely cured and saved the colonies by immersing them completely in straight tap water, chlo-rine, chloramines and all, for a five minute bath. As the colonies were for sale, and the presence of a dead side branch is esthetically unappealing, I cut the affected por-tions off during the bath. A large scissors works well for

*One minute is the rec-ommended duration for the freshwater dip.

this purpose. I make a cut in the top of the skeleton on one side just behind the damaged tissue and into healthy tissue, then I cut the opposite wall. Next, I open the scissors wide enough to make a bite that includes both cuts, and with slight pressure the skeleton breaks off cleanly. After the bath, the coral is placed back into an aquarium with good circulation, preferably a different aquarium to prevent re-infection with the protozoan, but I have had success as well with replacing the specimen in the same tank. It is to be expected that the coral will initially produce copious slime when returned to the tank. I have attempted freshwater baths with affected soft corals, so far with only limited success.

On the subject of treatments, there is one which I have been meaning to pass along to you which I hope will catch on with retail shops. It is a treatment for clownfish "white slime" disease. First, a little background about the scope of the problem. Certain clownfish species succumb to a massive infection within days after arrival at the pet shop, wholesale facility, or home aquarium. The symptoms are clamped fins, labored swimming and breathing, and production of a white slime secretion over the entire body. As the disease progresses, the slime becomes blotchy, and fins may become frayed. The fish may die within a day or two after the initial symptoms, or may last a week. Seldom does an affected fish recover. It is a common sight in a pet shop to find an aquarium with about twenty Ocellaris clowns all slimed up and with clamped fins. Ocellaris clowns from both Indonesia and the Philippines are the most frequently affected species, but the problem also affects the orange skunk clown, the saddle back clown, the fire clown, and the "black percula." While many shops have devised special treatments of their own incorporating formalin baths, freshwater dips, etc., I observed a very successful technique used at the Aquarium Center in Baltimore. Owner Dennis Hare showed me tanks with many completely healthy Ocellaris clowns, and told me of a quarantine procedure which he uses on them. It involves a three day stay in tanks with the following medications in the water: Furazone green light by Dynapet at the standard dosage. Chloremphenical at 250 mg/5 gallons, and methylene blue at 5-6 drops/gallon. Dennis cautions that this quarantine procedure does not preclude the incidence of other diseases, only the specific problem common to many clownfish. Loss of some of the clowns to protozoan infections during this quarantine procedure can occur, for instance.

I have found the treatment both simple and effective, and am recommending it here in the hope that it might save the lives of hundreds or perhaps thousands of these fish which are lost needlessly each year. I encourage input from the readers regarding their experience with this disease problem, and any especially effective remedies.*

*It is a good idea to give the clownfish a formalin dip first before treating with antibiotics, in order to knock out most protozoan parasites. See Moe's *The Marine Aquarium Handbook* for recommended procedure regarding the use of formalin.

One can no longer obtain such antibiotics from pet stores. They can be obtained from veterinarians. Substitute nitrofurazone for the Furazone green. CAUTION: chloremphenical and nitrofurazone are toxic to humans! Wear gloves and a dust mask when handling. Ask your veterinarian about other precautions. Be sure to aerate the treatment tank well since antibiotics lower the dissolved oxygen content of the water.

Reproduction Indicated... I wanted to make some additional comments about the mysterious black dots traveling up the tentacles of elegance coral, *Catalaphyllia jardinei*, which Jeff Joos photographed, and which appeared in my column in the July 1990 issue. Jeff wondered if his coral was trying to reproduce, and I indicated that I doubted this was the explanation, though I wouldn't rule it out. The reason I considered this possibility at all stems back to an observation made by John Burleson that *Anthelia* sp., a soft coral, releases eggs from the tips of its tentacles. Charles Delbeek wrote an article about the event, and it appeared along with John's photos in the March 1989 issue of FAMA.

At first I rejected Jeff's suggestion because it has been my experience and understanding that stony corals release eggs from the "mouth." Nevertheless, I am now compelled to agree that what Jeff Joos has observed are indeed eggs, as I recently witnessed a very unusual spawning event in an aquarium containing many Atlantic rock anemones, *Epicystis crucifer*. I was astonished to see eggs travel up to the trips of the tentacles in these anemones, while other anemones in the tank began pumping clouds of male gametes into the water from the pharynx.

Unfortunately, I didn't have my camera with me. Anemones are more closely related to stony corals than are the soft corals, and so it is possible that this method of reproduction has been retained by certain stony corals such as *Catalaphyllia*. I have a hunch that Mr. Joos' observation is an important one, and I encourage him to take more photographs and make careful notes on the occurrence. Now wouldn't it be interesting if he could obtain a male colony?

More On Calcium: I have been measuring calcium levels of sea water in the Miami area and have been getting values which are quite a bit higher than the standard 400 mg/L. Using a Hach Calcium test kit I have tested sea water at various locations and at different tides, and have found the level to be typically between 472 and 480 mg/L. In the reef aquaria I maintain I have measured values ranging from 350 mg/L to 448 mg/L. One must bear in mind that full strength sea water in the Miami area has a specific gravity of about 1.025, while most aquaria range between 1.020 and 1.023. This difference can account for some variation in the level of dissolved calcium. Still, I am curious about the potential benefits/disadvantages of maintaining elevated calcium levels in the aquarium. If the values which I have measured are accurate, then it could be recommended that calcium be maintained in excess of 450 mg/l. Calcium levels can fall pretty rapidly in a closed system with many calcium utilizing plants and invertebrates. In my own densely packed 15 gallon reef tank, for instance, the level can fall from 472 to 424 mg/l in a month, as measured with the same test kit. I have observed that some tanks maintain quite stable levels, in addition. Needless to say there is much still to be learned about calcium flux on the reef.

November 1990   Let's get through a stack of letters this month.

Q. I need some info on fire worms. One turned up in my salt tank. It's an invert tank with only one fish. So far the fire worm hasn't killed anything. It does come out a lot to feed when I feed the fish ... I put extra food down for it. I have two starfish, two urchins, three snails, one shrimp, four assorted crabs, a sea cucumber, and one anemone rock. The tanks is a 20 long and the worm is about 2-1/2 to 3 inches long. I had one before and I got rid of it, but thought I would keep this one. What should I feed it? What do I look for? How do they breed? Nothing seems to be afraid of it. The starfish and shrimp move right over it with no trouble from the worm. It's been here about four months. Rose Lunger, Bay City, Michigan

A. Well, Rose, I have talked about "fireworms" in a negative light in the past, and to be honest, I still don't care for 'em, but some clarification about them is in order since not all species of these bristly polychaetes are really harmful in the aquarium, and some hobbyists like yourself have indicated to me that they actually like them. I'm sure there are plenty of you out there who actually like liver too ... to each his own!

There is at least one species of fire or bristle worm that has an appetite for the tissue of cnidarians such as coral and anemones. It's name is *Hermodice carunculata,* which roughly translates to: "I eat coral so take me out of your minireef."

See the article about bristle worms by Dr. Ron Shimek, in the Summer 1994 issue of Aquarium Frontiers journal

I can't tell you exactly how to distinguish different types of bristle worms*, and I should point out that they all are omnivorous, so they may not sample your corals or anemones often or at all, for extended periods. *Hermodice* grows very large, and that is probably the best distinction I can offer. I have seen specimens on the reef in excess of a foot long — and that's no exaggeration — munching on zoanthid anemones. Many hobbyists have told me about the surprise discovery of a *Hermodice* at least ten inches long in their aquaria. I had such an experience myself about a year ago while I was siphoning detritus out from behind the reef. Although I had never noticed a bristle worm in my aquarium, all of a sudden a six inch long monster with a grin comes cruising along right where I was siphoning. Talk about timing! The worm didn't even have a chance to say, "Uh-Oh."

Rose's critter may be one of the smaller type which sift through the gravel for food. It was probably introduced with the "anemone rock." As far as feeding it, they eat just about anything, including fish waste, so there should be no fear of starvation. They reproduce by two methods. One method we all recall from grade school when our biology teachers showed us that the marriage of an earthworm and a knife could produce at least a couple of worms. Bristle worms divide either via accident or some biological cue, and they may do so quite frequently. I believe this is the principal method used which allows them to convert a gravel bed into worm city.

Polychaetes may also reproduce sexually, which involves swimming up into the water column to release gametes or, in some cases, the separation of a gamete-laden portion of the worm which swims into the water column only to spawn and die. Kind of a nifty way to avoid the risk of being eaten, but at the expense of missing all the fun.

Q. I am very interested in something you wrote about in "Reef Notes" July '90 issue. I would like to know specifics on setting up an aquarium using only a protein skimmer and live rock for filtration. How big does the protein skimmer need to be for the size of the tank? What are the best steps for setting the tank up, how long should you want to add fish and invertebrates?

I truly enjoy salt water tanks and this seems to be one of the most natural ways it can be done. If you have time could you possibly send a sketch of a good set-up?

Thanks for your time and effort. Also thanks for sharing your knowledge with the rest of us. Sincerely, Lance A. Bissell, Salem, Oregon

A. I'm glad I caught your interest on this subject. Since the method involves extensive explanation in order to properly present it, Charles Delbeek and I have prepared an article in which we present the concept, along with photographs of several aquaria utilizing different variations of the no-trickle-filter approach to reef keeping.* Naturally there are different schools of thought even among the segment of aquarists practicing this technique. Your questions will be answered in this article. I do not wish to be irresponsible in presenting an abbreviated explanation. You will just have to wait.

*Please see: Sprung, J.F. & J.C. Delbeek. 1990. "New trends in reef keeping." *FAMA* **13(12):8.**

Q. Ten months ago I started my very first aquarium, a 110 gallon reef tank. I built my own trickle filter but put a commercial protein skimmer, ozonizer, and lighting on it. It has had its ups and downs. I cycled the tank with 180 lbs. of live rock and have since added more for a total of 250+ lbs. I have the usual assortment of fish and invertebrates, and was plagued by hair algae and red slime algae. I went very slowly and overcame these problems. About three months ago I began to get a golden brown slime algae that got worse and worse. I siphoned it off but it would come back by each weekly water change. No one seemed to know what it was. The wet part of my trickle filter was crushed coral but when I stirred it up it emitted a foul odor and black residue. So I thought that I had read that a person had taken all his external biological medium out and ran the tank on the bacteria on the live rock, then I saw you mention the same thing in the July '90 Reef Notes. So out came the crushed coral and it was not replaced by anything else. I am happy to say the tank has never looked better. Within a three day period the corals blossomed, the anemones, are huge, but even more interesting is the fact that after one water change and the siphoning off of the golden slime it has not returned. It has been three weeks and still no sign of it. One question I have. You mention the German aquarist running his reef tank with no trickle filter at all, does that mean no dry portion (which I still have)? What about oxygenation of the water that takes place in the dry section or was this replaced by something else? Sincerely, Robert Crowther Washington, Massachusetts

A. If the aquarium has strong water motion, and there are no dead pockets such as your former wet section, or a thick gravel bed, then the oxygen level will be high even in the absence of a dry filter. The use of a protein skimmer can further elevate the level of dissolved oxygen by removing oxygen-scavenging compounds from the water. That black foul mess you experienced is the result of detritus accumulation and subsequent development of a healthy bed of anaerobic activity, which proceeded to the point of producing toxic hydrogen sulfide. Reduced iron gives the characteristic blackened appearance and the sulfide gives the odor of rotten eggs. You are lucky because a good dose of H_2S in the water will quickly kill most fish. The brown slime algae was probably a type of cyanobacteria, even though most "golden brown" looking algae are diatoms. In removing the wet media you removed a strong reducing "filter" from your system which was maintaining redox levels sufficiently low to allow ample availability of nutrients for the alga in question. It has been my experience that even when good prefiltration is used, a dense wet bed eventually becomes clogged and begins to be a drag on the oxygen level of the system, ultimately producing reducing compounds that lower redox potential. Nevertheless some professional hobbyists continue to use and recommend large, gravel-filled wet sections. While such aquarists may maintain successful aquariums with these wet filters, I cannot accept any claims that they are necessary or that something is lacking when they are removed.*

*This advice needs clarification because there are useful types of "wet filters". The wet filters I criticized here have the water passing through the gravel, which acts as both mechanical and biological filter. In later "Reef Notes" columns (and in the appendix in this book) I describe a method developed by Dr. Jean Jaubert, wherein gravel or sand are used either inside the tank or in attached aquaria that are essentially wet filters. The water does not flow through the substrate, however, only over it. The living sand bed effectively removes nitrate via denitrification, and when calcareous substrate is used it can replenish some calcium. See also: *The Reef Aquarium, Vol1* by Delbeek and Sprung.

I'm glad to hear from you about your experience, and I'm sure that your letter will benefit other hobbyists.

Q. In the wake of the San Francisco earthquake, I have a serious question to ask. How do I secure 500 plus pounds of aquarium (a 55 gallon tank) or larger, to prevent a total loss in the event of a quake? If I somehow attach this much weight to a wall, could this pull the all apart? Sincerely, Glen Williams, South Pasadena, California

A. Don sent me this letter, I guess under the assumption that I could answer it since I had an answer a while back for the guy in Colorado who wondered about lower atmospheric pressure affecting the level of dissolved oxygen in his planned reef tank. Look, I'm from Florida. I don't know from earthquakes ... hurricanes, maybe, but earthquakes, never!

Earthquakes ... now there's a real challenge to your reef-building skills! Assuming there was minimal damage in the home, one can imagine that there were plenty of hobbyists picking up the pieces of their fallen reef soon after the big quake.

To answer your question, Glen, (and no doubt my curiosity), I contacted an architect friend of mine who had a couple of suggestions. By the way, he said the wall idea was a bad one, but I could have told you that. He suggested two main possibilities that you could explore further. One is to use a shock absorbing system for the base of the aquarium, involving springs or a springy material such as neoprene. The other suggestion is suspension from the ceiling via cable connections in a hammock-like arrangement ... that ought to improve the appearance of your living room! My friend cautioned that the latter suggestion was risky, too, depending on the strength of your ceiling and the beams and walls that support it.

This question really is intriguing. Personally, I'd like to know what ingenious methods hobbyists have employed for this purpose in earthquake prone regions like California or Japan. Please write and let me know.

Q. I have been keeping fish since March 1989 and I am totally enthralled with this hobby.

My question concerns a miniature reef tank I have set up. It is currently stocked with a 1/2" percula clown and a 1/2" royal gramma. I am only starting, but would like some advice.

I made a wet/dry trickle filter on the lines of the "Bio-Logic" system. In the wet section I am using "Bio-Loks," as with the dry section. Is this acceptable?

It is a 35 gallon tank with 3/4" of crushed coral layering the bottom, a Hagen 400 powerhead powering the filtration system.

I added the product Biozyme when I put the fish in, however, I added this to the dry section on my filter. Should I have done this? There was a small trace of ammonia.

The lighting system will include two 2' actinic bulbs and two 2' Gro-Lux bulbs. Do you think this is too much lighting?

I am ready to purchase live rock, I believe. The tank tests no copper, pH is 8.4, 0.1 ppm ammonia, 0.0 ppm nitrite, and 0.0 ppm nitrate.

I would like to leave the rock unlit for about 3 weeks, as per your suggestion, but I can only add 25 to 30 lbs. because of my budget. What problems can I expect from later additions of rock?
I know this is rather pushing it, but I would also like to try and breed *Amphiprion ocellaris*. Would this tank, with dither fish, 16" height, and assembled in reef fashion be appropriate?

Thank you for putting up with this "shuffled" letter, but any help would be greatly appreciated. Sincerely, Jarrod Loerzer, Monmouth, Illinois

Q. Julian's observation: "Man who says he has one question for you really has many questions."

Well, since my answers to Mr. Loerzer's questions are coming long after he has gone ahead with his plans, I hope I can offer assistance to someone out there who might be wondering about some of the same things. I don't know what "Bio-Locks" are, but assuming they are inert and of sufficient surface area, then they are fine. I don't know if you've missed my comments on gravel for the bottom of reef tanks containing a large quantity of live rock, but I would recommend that you bring the level down to 1/4", remove the gravel altogether, or be sure not to have any behind and below the rocks, only in the front. This will assist you in preventing the accumulation of detritus which has a negative effect on the water quality.* It is not apparent in your letter how long the aquarium has been set up. Let's assume it is a new set-up. Based on the population of the tank, I would guess that it has fairly limited nitrifying capability. Adding live rock to a newly established tank with fish in it is a sure death sentence for the fish unless the rock is thoroughly "seeded," in which case it is harmless. Recognizing the difference between such safe rock and fresh rock which could expose your fish to potentially lethal doses of ammonia takes some experience. If the rock is thoroughly seeded, its addition will increase the nitrifying capacity of your aquarium, i.e., it will assist your filter. If the rock is fresh and fouling, the load could easily exceed the capacity of even the most thoroughly established filter, and nothing could save your fish except removal from the tank. Because it is far too complex a matter to describe all of the criterion I use to judge a rock's safety, I can best assist you in suggesting that you not add rock which has been in captivity for less than a month. Each piece of rock should be carefully observed for white slime sheets and blackened areas which, in combination with a sulfur "rotten egg" smell indicate fouling. When I put together a reef aquarium I add the rock first, and I do not add the fish until I am

*see my comments in the appendix and elsewhere regarding the management of live sand and bottom substrates.

certain that the tank is ready for them. Your questions about the proper procedure concern me and I do not think I can adequately cover all the ramifications with a general answer, so I am preparing a column in which I will describe the methods of setting up a reef tank that I recommend. (Naturally these methods will be the best because I think so!) Biozyme is useful in the establishment of a new aquarium and in the process of seeding live rock. The point of addition to the aquarium makes no difference, in my experience, though if you were attempting to assist fouling rocks, you would best add it directly to the tank.

Regarding your lighting plans, you will definitely not be over lighting the tank. On the contrary, I would recommend that you increase the lighting substantially. Look into obtaining high output tubes as I have discussed many times in this column, and understand that they require a special ballast ... I hope your budget permits.

Regarding your breeding aspirations, go for it! With proper food and regulation of the light and temperature you should be able to spawn them in no time. Dither fish are a freshwater standard, and are certainly not needed to make clownfish spawn.

Q. I have had a 55 gallon tank for about a year with trickle filter and six 40 watt fluorescent bulbs above it (four Actinic and two Daylight about 2" above the water, no UV shields, and no glass). The tank has six fish that have been together a long time — two cleaner wrasse, a strawberry basslet, a 3" Kole tang who refuses to eat the hairy algae I put him in there to eat, a clownfish that bites the hand that harvests algae from its tank, a yellow headed sleeper gobie, a fat 2" damsel, live rock (now mostly encrusted with microalgae and hair algae), and some long-time invertebrate residents which include feather dusters, an enormous pink *Condylactis,* a pink tip *Condylactis* (that shortly after entering the tank became a greenish-white with no pink tips), a fluorescent green-tipped anemone (that lost its green glow shortly after going into the tank and is now a drab brownish), and various rock anemones.

Water conditions are: salinity 1.023; temp. 75-78° F; phosphate .01 (I have had calcite in the wet chamber but am removing it slowly); nitrate was about 20 ppm (nitrate-n) two months ago, but has steadily dropped until now it is about 5 ppm; pH is 8.4; DKH is 15; copper .05 (SeaTest); ammonia and nitrite are 0.

Now for the problem, and it is a big one: As I said, I can't seem to kill off the microalgae, but I can kill off the corals. Twice I have mail ordered polyps and corals. The second try (eight months later) was the same as the first. I bought a *Cladiella* and acclimated it according to instructions. I placed it four inches from the top of the tank, in enough current to make it sway a bit. The next day and for the next three weeks it was fully opened and beautiful. In fact it was actually growing. However, I noticed the color darkening somewhat. I noticed one of the arms swollen, greyish, and its polyps unopened. The next day almost the whole animal looked the same way. Two days later it was shriveled, flopped over, coated with slime, and near death. The green polyps I ordered and placed about four inches from the top of the water also looked great for about the same amount of time. Now fewer and fewer are opening. I've moved them lower with the hope they might do better in less light. Likewise the blue mushroom anemones have all but shriveled up. The red ones were also starting to shrink, but seem to be holding their own near the bottom. The people I bought from suggested I do a 20% water change when I told them the mushroom anemones were going. I usually do a 2-1/2 gallon change per week, pick out any dying hair algae daily, and siphon off the hair algae to remove any dying particles as well.

A friend of mine regularly orders from the same mail order house and his purchases (including a *Cladiella*) are going great. Could I be having a problem with Ultraviolet light? I can get UV shields from the local lighting place, but is there not some toxin in my tank? I have a coral banded shrimp who is fine, but of the twelve *Turbo* sp. snails I put in, only three are alive (they are growing quite large, but won't consider eating hair algae). Thank you, Sandy Cohen, Albany, Georgia

A. No, Ultraviolet light is not the problem, though it bears some strong resemblance ... see last month's column. I suspect that your corals are getting burned by one or more wandering anemones. You have a lot of stinging anemones. The protozoan parasite, *Helicostoma*, can also cause similar symptoms, so it may be involved in your case. Lowering the salinity is the only recommendation I can make for *Helicostoma*. You will have to make a personal decision regarding the anemones. I feel certain that they are the problem. Have no fear about removing all of the calcite at once — it will improve your water quality, and help with your algae problem. I recommend that you purchase a small yellow tang to crop the hair algae down to a short fuzz that the *Turbo* snails and the Kole tang can work on. When the hair algae is too long they can't eat it.*

*I have plenty more to say about hair algae, not to worry. See the appendix. This aquarist could also try adding tiny red-legged or blue legged hermit crabs, which are excellent at grazing hair algae.

Are you using R.O. or deionized water? Avoiding the excess nutrients from tap or well water will also help with the algae problem. Good Luck!

Q. I am a 16 year old high school student who is crazy about aquariums. I have several tanks and have made several observations of fish behavior. The study of the symbiotic relationships between clownfish and anemones has always fascinated me. Currently I have a salt tank set up for a reef. In my own personal research, I have come upon something that I have never read about. I purchased a yellow carpet anemone (one of the carpets that is very sticky and a pain to the aquarist who gets one stuck on half of his hand), and a percula clownfish. The clownfish started to "chew" the tentacles of the anemone, not eat them. When the clownfish would move away, the tentacles were "deflated" of water. After about four hours I moved the carpet to the middle of the tank. I was surprised that it did not stick to my hand when I first touched it. It just felt slimy, similar to a sebae anemone. When I touched it several times in the process of moving it, it became sticky in the areas most touched. I have concluded that the clownfish put a mucus (or some other kind) of coating on the thread cells of the anemone, similar as it does to its body, supposedly. I do think that this has been noted before, but I have never read about it. I am writing this to you because I would like to share this information with others who might be interested. Thank you very much for your valuable time and I hope this information is helpful. Sincerely. David Byrd, Ft. Worth, Texas

A.: Hmmmmm ... interesting! While it is known that through a process of acclimation, anemonefish acquire a protein from the anemone and incorporate it in their own mucus to prevent the anemone's nematocysts from firing, I am not aware of any similar affect imparted to the anemone, as you suggest. Many aquarists, including yours truly, have noticed the curious and amusing habit these clowns have of chewing or sucking the tentacles. I always thought they did it for reasons kind of like the way people love to eat jalepeno peppers. Your perspective and suggestion shed a new light on the subject which would require careful analysis of the anemone's mucus to determine if such is the case that it is altered somehow. It might interest you, in addition, that clownfish often bite at the anemone when it brushes over their eggs. Personally I suspect that the clowns are fatiguing the anemone when they make the tentacles deflate, but I think your suggestion is definitely worth looking into.*

*For a much more detailed discussion of the relationship between anemones and clownfish, please read the book *Field Guide to Anemonefishes and their Host Sea Anemones* by Daphne Fautin and Gerald Allen.

Next month I will answer some more of your questions and, guess what? I have been getting pictures finally, so I'll be presenting some examples of reef aquaria run under different regimes. I will do this periodically so keep on sending them in.

Continued in the next *Reef Notes,* 2 (1991-92).

Appendix

There are some subjects that seem to demand advice over and over and over and over. I thought it would be a good idea to provide a condensed summary of advice for the most common questions I hear from reef keepers.

A more thorough treatment of these subjects can be found in *The Reef Aquarium, Vol 1.,* by Delbeek and Sprung.

Problem Algae
As one can see from the questions in this book, and from the ones in subsequent Reef Notes, the struggle with ugly growths of algae that rapidly smother everything is the number one problem. Every aquarist wants to know how to cure *MY SPECIAL CASE PROBLEM ALGAE.*

To eliminate red slime algae and other cyanobacteria
1. increase protein skimming. 2. increase water movement via powerheads and wave timers. 3. include tiny herbivorous hermit crabs. Red legged *Paguristes cadenati* and "blue legged" hermits, both from the Caribbean, stay under one inch and eat algae off the bottom substrate and rocks. 4. include bottom sorting creatures such as serpent starfish (approx. one per 5 gallons). These scavengers prevent the buildup of pockets of detritus, eat food that the fish miss and devour dead snails that would otherwise rot. 5. use filtered top off water (R.O. and/or deionized) 6. maintain pH at 8.4 during the day and above 8.0 at night via the addition of kalkwasser, dosed with a drip or level sensing dosing pump. 7. Eliminate mechanical filtration (on reef tanks...they are fine for fish tanks) such as sponges or cartridge cannister filters...these trap material that the protein skimmer would remove.

To eliminate hair algae
Do the same as above, but also employ herbivorous snails such as *Turbo* and *Astraea* (approx. one *Turbo* per 10 gallons or 1 *Astraea* per gallon...I prefer *Astrea* since they are smaller, but I also include some *Turbo*'s). The tiny hermit crabs are particularly good at eating hair algae, but one needs a lot of them to be effective...about one per gallon. *Zebrasoma* tangs (yellow, sailfin, purple) also are helpful in controlling hair algae, but they grow too large for small aquariums (less than 50 gallons).

To eliminate bubble algae (*Valonia* sp.).

In large aquariums adult *Zebrasoma desjardinii* will eat
Valonia. In small aquariums they are best managed by
picking them off the rock with a tweezers and removing
them from the aquarium. Strong growth of coralline
algae limits the growth of bubble algae.

To eliminate diatoms and dinoflagellates (brown algae)

Diatoms are controlled by limiting dissolved silicate in
the water, which they use to build their tiny skeletons.
Purified top-off water (R.O. and/or deionized) limits
their growth. Herbivorous snails also eat them. Similar
looking dinoflagellates, which bloom even in water with
low silicate, are characterized by rapid growth and
trapped oxygen bubbles in mucous strings and sheets.
They are usually brownish but may be almost colorless.
They can be stopped by elevating and maintaining the
pH at 8.4 or 8.5 via the addition of kalkwasser.
Siphoning them is futile since they grow back in hours.
They usually crash (die) after a few days at high pH.

Aiptasia

Those darned anemones that take over the tank can be
controlled. Old advice suggests using fish that eat them
such as the copperband butterfly *Chelmon rostratus* or
the raccon butterfly, *Chaetodon lunula*. Peppermint
shrimp (*Lysmata wurdemani*) also will prey on *Aiptasia*,
as will some angelfish. The fish may also eat other invertebrates that you don't want them to eat, and when you
remove the fish the *Aiptasia* return since the fish merely
prune the anemones and don't really eliminate them.
Injecting the anemones with different chemicals or boiling water works when small numbers of anemones are
present, but this method is impractical if there is a
plague of them. The best technique was suggested to me
recently by John Brandt. John noticed that an "*Aiptasia*
free zone" seemed to exist around Elegance coral,
Cataliaphyllia jardinei. He then tried brushing the
anemones with the tentacles of an elegance coral and
found that after several days of exposure to the coral
tentacles the anemones died. I tried this and found it
works well. The tentacles should make full contact with
the anemone(s) for just a few minutes per day for several
consecutive days. Other aquarists have since noticed

that the stony coral *Hydnophora excesa* also is lethal to *Aiptasia*. Some specialized nudibranchs also eat them. See: *The Reef Aquarium Vol 1.*

Live Sand

All materials placed in the aquarium become coated, encrusted, and populated by a variety of bacteria, microorganisms, and algae. Submerged sand, gravel, rocks, etc. therefore become "live." Sand and rocks collected in the natural environment contain stable communities of bacteria, micro and macro-organisms. Aquarists have learned that innoculating their aquariums with these substrates rapidly produces a stable environment. The bacteria and microorganisms play an important role in biological filtration as they digest organic and inorganic waste produced by the fish and invertebrates. Live sand has been promoted lately for the purpose of establishing a natural, in-tank denitrifying filter (see diagrams and description of Dr. Jaubert's method).

Kalkwasser

I recommend that you use calcium hydroxide in the top-off water. In my opinion the best way to administer it is with an automatic water top-off system employing a level sensing switch to control a pump for dosing. It is also best to have a pH meter to judge the proper dosage. Further information about the use of Kalkwasser and comparisons to other methods are given in *The Reef Aquarium, Vol 1.*

pH

If I were to give a complete explanation of pH here you might get scared out of the water, so I won't. Please see the references at the end of this appendix for further information about pH. The pH of the water refers to how acidic or alkaline it is. Many times I have heard the remark that marine aquariums are so difficult to keep because you have to keep adjusting the darned pH to keep it right. I imagine the origin of this statement has to do with too much emphasis on testing the water with pH kits. In fact, the pH naturally fluctuates from day to night as a result of respiration (at night) when it falls and photosynthesis by plants during the day, when it rises. Therefore a range of readings over the course of the day is normal, and a single test may not mean very much. The acceptable pH range for tropical marine fish is between 7.6 and 8.5. The normal range is between 7.9 and 8.4. Invertebrates prefer to be within the latter range. When the pH tends to be low, it is an indication either that the tank is holding too much carbon dioxide or that the buffer is depleted by the acid released in nitrification. If aeration of the water brings the pH up, the former problem is demonstrated. The solution is better circulation to release the excess CO_2. The latter problem with pH is more common, and it is resolved with the addition of kalkwasser or buffer, water change, and via the natural process of denitrification.

Gas exchange

When I refer to gas exchange I'm not talking about meetings of OPEC nations nor the effect of a bean burrito with onions, I mean how oxygen and carbon dioxide pass into and out of the aquarium. Though it contains a whole community of life, the aquarium can be viewed as a single living organism that must breathe and respire. Wider tanks afford better gas exchange than taller tanks because they have a larger water/air interface for the given water volume. If you're smart you'll choose a tank with the front to back dimension equal to or greater than the height.

Chemical filtration

The use of activated carbon, while not essential, is a common practice for removing organic compounds that turn the water yellow. It is a simple mater to include a bag of activated carbon in a power or cannister filter, in the sump, or within the aquarium in a place where water is generally drawn through or over it. *Forcing* the water through it can cause the grains to tumble and crumble, emitting dust into the tank. Some aquarium literature suggests that ideal use of activated carbon involves directing the water through it in a packed column. This makes sense, and I agree it is the *most efficient* way to use it to filter the water. Nevertheless, *for reef aquariums* I recommend passive use of activated carbon, described above, to avoid too rapid a depletion of trace elements while still keeping the water from becoming yellow.

Redundancy in pumps

The pumps utilized to move the water are like the beating heart of the living aquarium. If you rely on one pump only, its failure when you're on vacation could leave you with a broken heart and a smelly mess. For this reason I recommend redundancy of pumps, which greatly reduces the likelihood of such a preventable tragedy. One may simply use an air driven diffuser inside the aquarium as a backup to the recirculating water pump, or additional powerheads, or just two recirculating pumps.

Some Simple Systems

The systems I recommend have as common virtues low cost, low maintenance, and low probability of failure. When asked what I feel is the simplest set up for maintaining fish and or invertebrates I can't help but think of Lee Chin Eng's natural system. Basically all you need is the tank, some limestone rocks (preferrably at least some live rock), gravel or sand on the bottom, and strong circulation from an air driven diffuser* or water pumps (see diagram). The light can be from a window if temperature is not a problem, or it can be from artificial lamps. I have seen successful modifications using a hang on the back powerfilter for additional circulation and chemical filtration, or external cannister filters for the same purpose. If you've never kept an aquarium before, you will become hooked if you try a simple natural system with a couple of pieces of live rock. You will be amazed by the incredible variety of living things that crawl out of the rock or grow from it. Many people have been astonished to realize that they have been staring at the life in their little five or ten gallon aquarium for over an hour. What you have really is a sort of miniature world or universe.

A simple quarantine system.

Patience is waiting a couple of weeks before putting the new fish into the display tank, while the new fish is in another tank in quarantine. What, another tank? A quarantine tank is a useful tool for preventing the incidence of disease epidemics in the display tank. Public aquariums typically follow a rigorous, lengthy quaranine procedure, involving a sequence of drug treatments to eliminate the most common diseases. The quarantine procedure I am proposing does not render the fish disease free, however. It merely allows the fish to become acclimated to captivity in a calm environment where no other fish are bullying it after the stressful ordeal of capture and transportation has already weakened it. The quarantine period builds up the fish's strength and natural immunity to disease.

I set up a quarantine tank in nearly the same manner as Eng's system. It is like a miniature display tank. Psychologically this is helpful to both the fish and the aquarist because the quarantine tank looks at least like a second display tank. It does not have permanent fish residents, however. For quarantine I recommend either a 10 or 20 gallon tank set up with several well-aged pieces of live rock, an air diffuser, and a small heater. I generally leave the bot-

*Airstones produce fine bubbles which effect some protein skimming along the walls of the tank. They also produce salt spray and salt creep. Therefore it may be preferrable to use an open ended bubbler, although they can be noisier. Open ended rigid airline can also become clogged with dust, salt and minerals...it is wise to include supplemental water motion from a powerhead or powerfilter.

Modified Eng's Natural System. (not to scale)

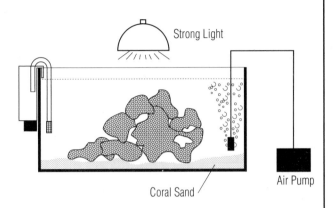

Strong Light

Coral Sand

Air Pump

A simple quarantine tank. (not to scale)

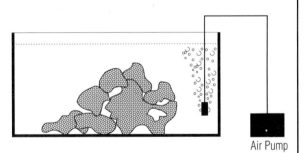

Air Pump

tom of the quarantine tank bare. I maintain the temperature the same as the display tank. I put a lid on to keep the fish from jumping out and reduce evaporation, and the light may be ambient daylight from a window, stray light from the display tank, or from a dedicated fixture. I prefer to quarantine one fish at a time. It is possible to have several together, but all must remain in quarantine for at least two weeks. Any fish added late necessitates restarting the two week clock.

If after two weeks in the quarantine tank a fish does not develop disease symptoms, is actively eating, and appears "spunky," it is ready to be introduced into the display tank. Moving the fish again is stressful to it, and introduction to the display tank often involves aggression from the old residents. To minimize this effect it can be helpful, though not essential, to follow one more procedure. Find a clear plastic container with a screw-on lid and drill holes in the sides for circulation. Capture the quarantined new fish in this container, screw on the lid. Place the caged fish in the display tank, secured in place perhaps with a rubber band and a rock. Keep it this way for one or two days, without food. The old residents will see the new fish and vent their aggression without being able to beat it up. Surprisingly, this release of "tension" without the possibility of injury seems to make the new fish more confident and the old residents less likely to bother it when it is released.

If the fish develops disease symptoms in the quarantine tank, it must be treated. This appendix is meant as an overview and cannot cover the range of diseases and treatments, but I have provided at the end a list of references for that purpose. When treatment in quarantine is necessary, I remove the live rocks and place them in a bucket of sea water with airation to keep them alive, because the chemicals used to treat diseases often are lethal to organisms in the rock. I medicate the fish in the now bare aquarium. For shelter I give the fish some short lengths of PVC pipe. When the fish has recovered and is without disease symptoms for a period of more than two weeks, it may be moved to the display aquarium.

Selecting hardy fish: ones to avoid

One of the greatest secrets to success with marine fish is knowing which ones to choose. By this I do not refer to the ability to pick healthy fish. What I mean is knowing which fish have the least propensity to get sick and die in an aquarium. I like fish that don't die too easily. The following fish are least likely to contract the common diseases *Cryptocaryon* and *Amyloodinium*. Hawkfish, including the Flame hawk, Arc Eye, and Longnose hawkfish;

Basslets, including Royal Gramma, *Pseudochromis* species; Cardinalfish such as the Pajama Cardinal; and tank- raised clown-fish. There are many more hardy fish that are suitable for reef aquariums, but I just wanted to point out ones that are the safest.

The wrath of Tang

Probably the most significant cause of chronic disease problems in reef aquariums, tangs are very prone to *Amyloodinium* and *Cryptocaryon*. Since they are among the best herbivorous fishes, most aquarists include at least one species of them in a reef aquarium. Not only are they prone to disease, they also tend to make other fish sick. Some species are more prone to getting sick than others. Avoid *Ctenochaetus* spp., such as the Kole and Chevron tang, and also avoid *Acanthurus* species such as the Powder blue and Achilles tang. The *Zebrasoma* species are the most disease resistant, and they are good grazers. Feed them often to keep them fat!

Fish disease in a reef tank

The occurrence of disease in a reef tank is troublesome because the medications typically used in fish-only tanks (or in quarantine) to eradicate protozoan parasites or cure bacterial infections also kill the invertebrates and beneficial bacteria respectively if used in a reef tank. The most common question concerns the incidence of "ich" or white spot disease. Aquarists often use the term "ich" to describe both the condition caused by the protozoan parasite *Cryptocaryon irritans*, and the condition caused by the dinoflagel-late *Amyloodinium*. The latter disease is commonly cauled marine velvet.

New aquarists often simply do not understand the life cycle of the parasites that affect fish. Many parasites encyst on the fish and then drop off and reproduce on the bottom of the aquarium. When they drop off, the fish appears to have recovered for a day or so. This cycle leaves the impression that something the aquarist did cured the condition, when in fact it didn't. For this reason unaware aquarists may praise the "effect" of magic cures. Please don't be fooled!

Curing "ICH" without medications

I have found that simply dropping the specific gravity of the reef aquarium to about 1.016 or 1.017 for extended periods is most effective in curing *Cryptocaryon*. **Please note:** When lowering the specific gravity, which is accomplished by taking out some salt water and diluting the system with freshwater over a period of a

Other Suggested Readings

Brandenburg, W. 1968. Filtration of marine aquaria. T.F.H. 17(4): 4-17.

Emmens, C.W. 1975. *The Marine Aquarium in Theory and Practice.* T.F.H. Publications, Neptune City, New Jersey.

————— 1986. The natural system and the minireef. Freshwater and Marine Aquarium 9:71.

Eng, L.C. 1961. Nature's system of keeping marine fishes. T.F.H. 9(6):23-30.

————— 1976. Stop killing the corals. Marine Hobbyist News 4(8):5.

Jaubert, J. and J.P. Gattuso, 1989. Changements de forme provoques par la lumiere, observes, en aquarium, chez coraux (Scleractiniaries a zooxanthelles). Deuxieme Congres International d'Aquariologie 1988 Monaco, 1989. Bull. de l'Institut Oceanagraphique, Monaco, No. special 5:195-204.

—————, 1989 An Integrated nitrifying-denitrifying biological sys

few hours, **also add buffer to keep the alkalinity up**. If one does not add buffer, the alkalinity and pH of the aquarium water could drop too low. Maintain the alkalinity at 2.5 milliequivalents (7 dKH) or higher during the period that the specific gravity is reduced. When the fish have been without symptoms of Ich for two weeks, one may begin to add salt mix to the make up water to SLOWLY bring the specific gravity back up to a more typical level of 1.020 to 1.025. The lowered specific gravity technique is most effective with *Cryptocaryon,* but is less effective with *Amyloodinium,* though it can help the fish build strength to fight it. At lower specific gravity fish expend less energy in the process of osmoregulation.

Inverts to avoid

Most nudibranchs (they starve) "Medusa worm" sea cucumber (it is toxic to fish) Sea Apple (can be toxic to fish but otherwise OK if kept without fish).

Jaubert's method

Dr. Jaubert of the University of Nice, France and the Oceanographic Museum in Monaco places the bottom substrate on a platform that elevates it off the bottom of the aquarium. The purpose of this elevation is to create underneath the live sand a boundary layer pocket of water with very little surface area for the growth of microorganisms. This way the oxygen level beneath the sand approaches 1ppm but is less likely to fall to zero than it would be if the sand were directly on the bottom. A second screen prevents burrowing fish or invertebrates from disturbing the lower sand layer. The biological activity on the high surface area of the sand lowers the oxygen level, and bacteria within it effectively convert nitrite and nitrate to nitrous oxide and nitrogen gas while consuming organic matter. Their activity also generates calcium from dissolution of the sand by respired CO_2 and alkalinity from the breakdown of organic matter. It is important to have high oxygen levels above the sand (via water circulation and photosynthesis).

Bob Goemans and Sam Gamble have written about their experimentation with this method in *Marine Fish Monthly, Freshwater and Marine Aquarium*, and in *Aquarium Frontiers* (in press) Gamble presents an analysis of the oxygen levels and migration of substances through the sand layers. I have included some diagrams here to suggest a couple of ways that one could utilize Dr. Jaubert's living substrate approach to biological filtration and elimination of nitrate. Please bear in mind that the diagrams are schematic only, not blueprints. I build the platform from eggcrate

Jaubert System in an external sump.
(not to scale)

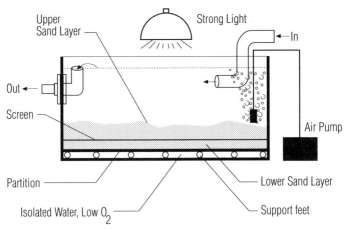

Upper Sand Layer

Strong Light

In

Out

Screen

Air Pump

Partition

Lower Sand Layer

Support feet

Isolated Water, Low O_2

Jaubert System in an external sump incorporated into an existing system. (not to scale)

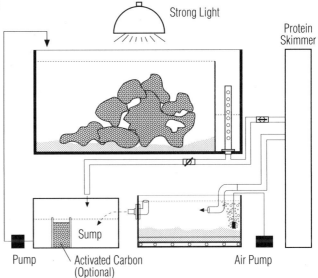

Strong Light

Protein Skimmer

Pump

Sump

Activated Carbon (Optional)

Air Pump

tem capable of purifying seawater in a closed circuit system. In: Deuxieme Congres International d'Aquariologie (1988) Monaco. Bulletin de l'Institut Oceanographique, Monaco, No. special 5:101-106.

—————————, 1991. U.S. Pat. no. 4,995,980.

—————————,

Pecheux, J-F., Guschemann, N., and F. Doumenge. 1992. Productivity and calcification in a coral reef meso-cosm. in Proceedings of the 7th International Coral Reef Symposium, in press.

Nilsen, A. J. 1990. The successful coral reef aquarium: part 3. Freshwater and Marine Aquarium 13(11):32

————————— 1991. Coral reef vs. reef aquarium: Part 2. Aquarium Fish Magazine 4(1):18-26.

Paletta, M. 1993. Enemies in the invertebrate aquarium. Aquarium Fish Magazine 5(7):18-26.

Riseley, R.A. (1971). *Tropical Marine Aquaria: The Natural System.* Allen and Unwin, London.

cut to fit the inside dimensions of the tank. Cut the platform in half so that it can be installed easily. Three layers of plastic window screening cut to the size of the plate and secured to the eggcrate with small plastic cable ties prevent the sand from falling through. Feet to support the weight of the sand are made from cut sections of 1" pvc pipe or from 3/4" couplers. The feet are attached horizontally to the eggcrate plate with cable ties. One can include this design inside the reef aquarium or, for already established aquariums, one can build a refugium sump with live sand, as shown in the diagram, and incorporate it in the system. One suggested location is given. Note that although Dr. Jaubert's original descriptions do not cover protein skimming, he is not opposed to its use. I have incorporated it in the diagram to show how it can fit in the system.

Choosing a protein skimmer.

Choose a skimmer that can process at least the entire volume of the aquarium in one hour. If it can handle more flow without sending bubbles back into the tank or onto the floor, great. External skimmers should have a large pipe returning water to the tank or sump, and a tall, not-too-constricted neck to allow good foam drying. Note installation of skimmers in the diagrams. They are fed surface skimmed water from the overflow drain.

Other modified "natural systems"

With this system there is no sump, no overflow to lose fish over, no holes through the wall, and no plumbing. An internal skimmer is used and water make-up can be achieved with a level switch placed in the tank to control a dosing pump in a freshwater reservoir below the tank.

The last piece of advice I can offer is to read some good books. I recommend the following texts: Moe's *Marine Aquarium Handbook* and *Marine Aquarium Reference* from Green Turtle Publications, and Tullock's *Successful Saltwater Aquariums Volume 1.* from Coralife. For information on invertebrates see: Wilkens' and Birkholz's *Marine Invertebrates* two volume set and Delbeek and Sprung's *The Reef Aquarium Volume 1.* Also see the video, "An Introduction to the Hobby of Reef Keeping" by Julian Sprung. For information on diseases see Moe's *Marine Aquarium Handbook* and *Aquariology Master Volume: The Science of Fish Health Management* published by Tetra Press. Additional suggested readings are in the margin. More will be given in subsequent volumes of this series pertaining to the subject matter of the "Reef Notes" columns contained in them.

**External Protein
Skimmer Setup.**
(not to scale)

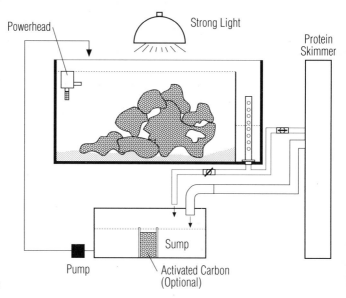

Powerhead

Strong Light

Protein
Skimmer

Sump

Pump

Activated Carbon
(Optional)

**Internal Protein
Skimmer Setup.**
(not to scale)

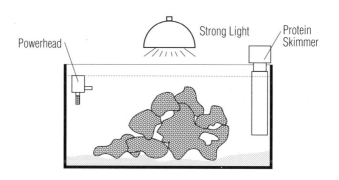

Powerhead

Strong Light

Protein
Skimmer

You should be able to find this book in your local library, book store, aquarium shop, pet store, or public aquarium. If you cannot find it locally, please send a self addressed stamped envelope to:

Ricordea Publishing, c/o Two Little Fishies, Inc., 4016 El Prado Blvd., Coconut Grove, Florida, USA, 33133, or call: Tel (305) 661-7742, Fax (305) 661-0611, hours 9 AM to 6 PM Eastern Standard Time, Monday thru Friday.